Mammy Val's Little Book of 'All-Sorts'

Val Baker Addicott

'Mammy Val's Little Book of Allsorts'

Copyright © 2014 Val Baker Addicott

All rights reserved.

ISBN:-10: 1500207586

ISBN-13: 978-1500207588

Val Baker Addicott

DEDICATION

To my daughter Eryl Lynne and to all her friends who refer to me as
'Mammy Val'
Hence the title of the book

'Mammy Val's Little Book of Allsorts'

CONTENTS

Short Stories:-

Page:-

1-23	The House on the Hill
39-61	Me and my Big Foot
101-151	Merlin
177-208	Over the Garden Wall

Poetry:-

Page:-

25	Today by Ella Wheeler Wilcox
27	Requiem – By Robert Louis Stevenson
28	Sea Fever – By John Mansfield
29	Time you old Gypsy-man By Ralph Hodgson
31	Upon Westminster Bridge - By William Wordsworth
32	Creeds – By Ella Wheeler Wilcox
32	The Reaper – By William Wordsworth
34	Elegy – By Thomas Gray
42	Verses from Hiawatha - By Henry W Longfellow

152	A Birthday – By Christina Rossetti
153	Someone Who Cares – By Edgar Guest
154	The Vicar of Bray
157	Reputation – By William Shakespeare
158	On First looking into Chapman's Homer - By John Keats
159	The Glory of the Garden - By Rudyard Kipling
160	The Rainbow – By William Wordsworth
160	Little White Road
161	I Wandered Lonely as a Cloud - By William Wordsworth
163	I Will Make You Brooches - By Robert Louis Stevenson
209	In Flanders' Fields – By Major John McCrae
210	Lest we Forget
210	Ecclesiastes Chap. 3 – verses 1-8
212	Alchemy of a Woman
213	1 Corinthians 13 – King James Version
214	The Gate of the Year – Marie Louise Haskins
215	Footprints Prayer
217	Morte D'Arthur – By Alfred – Lord Tennyson
218	Polonius' Advice to his Son – By William Shakespeare
219	Mercy – By William Shakespeare

220	Yours - By Leo Marks
221	Unchained Melody – By Hy Zanet
222	Union Song – The Bells of Rhymney – By Idris Davies
223	A Dog's Will and Testament
224	Jerusalem –By William Blake

Saying & Words of Wisdom – 164-167

Native American Sayings - 40

Recipes:- Page 73

Page:-

74	Gran's Puzzle Pudding
75	Leek & Potato Soup
76	Glamorganshire Sausages
77	Variations on a theme of Bread & Butter Puddings
78	Gran's Christmas Trifle
79	Black Forest Trifle
79	Gran's Christmas Cake

81	Special Vitamin Broth
82	Hot Weather Medicine
83-93	Old fashioned remedies and 'cure all'.

Wines:-

94	Rhubarb Wine
95	Hock Wine
95	Elderberry Port
96	Elderberry Wine
97	Another Elderberry Wine
97	Blackberry Wine
98	Blackberry Cordial
98-99	Gran's Hints on Wine making

Chutneys:-

169	Home-made Piccalilli
170	Indian Chutney
170	Mustard Ketchup
171	Mustard Pickle
171	Tomato Chutney
172	Tomato Sauce
172	Apple Chutney

173	Marrow Chutney

Something Different:-

173	Ox Heart Pudding
173	Pigs' Feet Pie
174	Nourishing Soup & Jelly
174	Poor Man's Goose
174	White Soup
175	Rabbit Brawn

Dodie's Letters Home 1941/46

225-300	An evacuee's letters
301	**The D'Alroy Diary – Why Hurry**

Note: Have tried to get page numbers correct just hope they don't change in printing.

'Mammy Val's Little Book of Allsorts'

Val Baker Addicott

Val Baker Addicott

ACKNOWLEDGMENTS

A big 'THANK YOU' to
David Redd for all his encouragement and all the hard work he put into scanning Dorothy's letters.

'Mammy Val's Little Book of Allsorts'

THE HOUSE ON THE HILL

THE END

"Well that's the end of her; she has been a worry to Dora ever since she went to that house; come on Joe let's go and have a pint with the others before we head home."
"Not a very good 'turn-out' for her; by the way what are you going to do with the house? It should fetch quite a bit or will you rent it; but I suppose it will be better to sell it to a stranger as no local would want to live in that 'God-forsaken hole'. Is it true what everyone is saying that she drowned?"
"Yes, it has been assumed that she was going to market in the horse and trap and the bridge collapsed and she got thrown out into the deluge of the flood waters; the funny thing is the horse managed to get to the other side. A bit mysterious if you ask me. As for the house I don't know what is going to happen as we were surprised that her solicitor is coming at four to read the will; I hope the stupid bitch hasn't done anything daft."
Hiding in the bushes that surrounded the grave-side she started to laugh; 'stupid bitch am I; just you wait Peter

Walker and you will find out how clever I really am.'

"Where the hell did that wind come from?" said Peter turning up his jacket collar.

"What wind? I didn't feel anything there isn't even a breeze; they say it is the hottest July we've had for years."

'I'll show them', she thought and passing close to the two men she gave out a raucous laugh.

'You are right Pete I felt it then;' he too turned up the collar of his jacket as she continued to laugh.

"My God Joe she has come back to haunt us; there isn't a quiver of the leaves on the trees yonder. Let's get the hell out of here."

"Now you are being an idiot; she dead and buried and there are no such thing as ghosts. It is just a fluke wind."

Once more she circled around them and following them down the path that led from the grave-side she darted in between them and blew in their faces a cold breath; 'see you later my dear brother-in-law; you are in for a big shock; might give you a heart-attack and then you will be joining me.'

"My, it has turned cold; I feel a sudden chill. Let's go and have a few pints."

"Perhaps we are in for a storm but what amazes me there isn't a cloud in the sky."

Once again emitting a cold breath over them she circled around and saying; 'I'll be waiting for you Peter Walker I just can't wait to see your face when my will is read;' she left them and transported herself to her sister's home.

"I hate grave-yards; the very thought of all those dead bodies lying in their crypts really scares me; wouldn't want to be here at night-fall when they say the dead walk."

"Shut up; you silly old fool, they are dead as door-nails you've been reading too many of those 'Penny Dreadful' stories."

Back at her sister's home she placed herself on the fender of the newly black-leaded grate; 'my house-proud sister' she thought; for as long as she could recall her sister would only light a fire in the parlour at Christmas time. 'Hope she won't light one today or I will be in a very hot place but there I am sure that is where she will be wishing me by the end of the afternoon.' She laughed at her own humorous thought.

"Has some-one left the back door open I just felt such a draft?" Said old granny Walker as she contentedly rocked away in Peter's favourite chair.

"Don't be silly mother-in-law it is absolutely boiling in here."

"I'd like a drink; a nice bottle of stout and hurry up with it girl."

"We're waiting for the men; you know they have to be served first."

"My Peter wouldn't deprive his mother of a bottle of

stout; hurry along girl or I will die of thirst and it is so hot in here there's not a breath of air think we're in for a storm."

"No pleasing the silly old bat she just said there was a draft and now she is complaining she's hot; once we get Sylvia's money Peter and I are off; we're going to get a nice little cottage by the sea-side." Dora said to her neighbour. "See how she'll cope without us."

'The old bat has hit the nail on the head', thought Sylvia as she perched herself on the back of the rocking chair; 'there certainly is a storm brewing'. In a jovial mood she began to make the rocking chair move faster on its rockers; how she would have liked to have tipped the old woman, whom she had always detested, onto the hearth. Instead she blew cold air down the back of her neck.

"Someone has left that door open again; there is a hell of a draft here."

"It is only me mother and the lads; we stopped off for a pint and on the way up the hill we met the solicitor." Said Peter as he entered the room

"Did you bring me a bottle of stout; I asked Dora ages ago and she said I couldn't have one."

"You can drink stout all day long, mother dear, after the will is read. We should have a nice packet from the sale of that house. Come on lads let's get to the table and tuck in all of you. Let's drink a toast to the bitch who is going to make us rich." He raised his glass and just as he said. "To the bitch", she bumped his arm and the ale tipped down his best suit and over the white table cloth. He turned to his wife, who was pouring Joe a cup of tea; "watch what you doing you clumsy woman good thing it wasn't boiling tea."

"I was nowhere near you; it is you who are the clumsy one been drinking too much again. I'll be glad to get you away from your old cronies."

How Sylvia longed to tip up the tea-pot down Dora's best dress but that might cause a serious accident so instead she turned her attention back to Peter who was trying to mop up the tipped ale. 'Want another bottle?' she breathed over him but this time her breath was hot and it made Peter's face redden and in the next instant she brushed against the bottle of ale he had just opened and up-tipped it into his lap.

"You clumsy oaf," shouted his wife; "I just had your suit cleaned and look at the mess you've made."

Joe burst out laughing; "Pete can't hold his liquor he has just wet himself."

He tried to get up but Sylvia now sat on his shoulder and with every attempt she pushed him back.

He turned to his friend Joe; "She is here Joe I can feel her presence; I didn't tip that bottle."

"You need to see a shrink old pal; we just buried her so how can she possibly be here?"

"I didn't mean *her;*" he stressed the word; "I mean her spirit; I can feel her all around me."

'Dare she', thought Sylvia but she didn't think about it for long and with an extra effort she pulled the chair from under Joe and as she roared with laughter her breath exhaled across the two men and Dora; sending a chill that made them shiver.

"Told you," said Peter; "I told you she was here."

As the old grand-father clock struck the hour of four the solicitor rose from his chair and tapping on his empty glass with a fork he said; "I am here on the request of Miss Sylvia Roberts to read her last will and testament." He sat back down and moving the plates and cutlery he picked up his brief case, that he had placed on the floor by the side of his chair; opening it he took out a single sheet of paper.

"Not much on that paper Dora, my love, our fortune awaits us."

The solicitor lowered his glasses on his nose and glared at Peter with his bird-like eyes; "May I continue? It will not take me long and I will be away. The will is very simple."

"Just like her," muttered Dora and quickly put her hand to her face as she felt a sharp pain in her ear.

'Simple am I just you wait Dora Walker.'

"As I was saying."

"Well spit it out man we're wasting good drinking time."

"Miss Roberts has left all her estate in the hands of her solicitors Dobson, Dobson and McIntire to be used at their discretion in the upkeep of Hill House for it to be maintained as it was on her demise. There is a clause that she has requested must not be read but acted upon when the time arises. I will now bid you 'Good day'." Closing his briefcase and picking up his hat off the coat hook he made his departure.

'Now for the thunder-storm', thought Sylvia. It wasn't long in coming; soon the air was blue and how she laughed when they wished her to suffer long and join the devil in Hades. She swirled around the room like a puff of smoke and tipping up a plate of sandwiches a few more bottles of beer and dropping a cream cake on old granny Walker's best silk dress she made her departure and returned to the house on the hill and to her beloved where they would at last be united. She hadn't planned her death but like everything that had happened over the last decade her destiny had been planned. It was fated that they would be together and now as two spirits their happiness was complete and they would never be disturbed in the house they loved so much and she had made sure that when the time was right they would open their doors to another such lost soul as she had been.

THE BEGINNING

"Isn't it about time you got yourself a man? Peter and I would like some privacy and not have you listening in to all our conversation and everything else; I have just about had enough; we've also got to put up with the old woman."
"I have as much right to be here as you; mother left the house to both of us."
"That was before I got married. As newly-weds we need time to ourselves; we'll never have kids with you listening in it really puts Pete off. If you can't get yourself a man for goodness sake get a job; it was okay when you were caring for old Mrs. Tucker."
"Well, we knew she wouldn't live for-ever; she was nearly ninety when I went to care for her. So tell me, *dear sister*" she made a point of emphasizing the words; "where did you expect me to live after her death?"
"Go and make yourself useful; it is Monday and I have a pile of washing to do as that old hag has wet her bed again."
Sylvia picked up the laundry basket and leaving her sister still complaining went to peg out the clothes. As she hung the clothes on the garden line she mulled over her sister's words. She really did hate living here; between old granny Walker constantly complaining and unable to sleep at night listening to the moaning and groaning

coming from the next room and the rattling of the old bedstead. What they were up to every night left very little to the imagination.

The washing hung out to dry; her bedroom tidied and not feeling up to any more arguments with her sister she decided to take herself off to the next town to see if she could find a job as she was now beginning to feel that if she didn't her sister would take action and kick her out and that would surely mean the work-house for her.
"I'm off out; anything you need?"
"Yes, you out of this house; if you know what is good for you don't bother to come back."

To save on the bus fare she decided to take the mountain road to the next town; some five miles distant, as the crow flies. The route was familiar to her so she couldn't understand, on seeing a house she had never previously noticed, how she could have taken the wrong path that had taken her up a rather steep hill. Feeling quite exhausted she sat on a bolder and took in the panoramic view of the surrounding country-side. Surely, from this vantage point she would be able to see the next town but all she could see was field after field of grazing sheep and cows and a few distant farm-houses and the river winding its way to the sea.

"Good-morning young lady; I thought you might be thirsty so I brought you a beaker of ice cold spring water from the well."

Sylvia had been deep in thought and was startled on hearing a voice. She turned and saw standing behind her an elderly lady whose mode of dress was different, to say the least. It was as if she hadn't moved into the twentieth century as her dress was early Victorian. Sylvia took the beaker of water and thanked the lady.

"Do you live in the house on the hill?" she questioned.

"Yes I have always lived there."

"How do you manage to do your shopping living so far from the town?" Sylvia felt that the lady appeared too fragile to travel far."

"I manage well; I have friends and we need very little."

Later, recalling that moment, Sylvia didn't know what had made her ask; "do you need someone to live-in and care for you?"

"Why do you ask, my dear?"

"My sister wants me to move out and if I don't find a job it will mean the work-house for me."

"Destiny has sent you here and I am sure I can speak for the others but we would love you to come and live with us. Return to us on Midsummer's Day and we will welcome you."

"How will I find this place again?"

"The spirits will guide you."

Refreshed from the pure, clear water and her rest upon the boulder Sylvia thanked the lady and promised to return on the 21st June. That would give her just a few days to make the necessary arrangements for her move. Happily, she began to make her way down the hill and turning to wave to the lady she noticed that she had been joined by a few other people all wearing different attire as if they were a troop of travelling actors.

On her arrival home there was no welcome awaiting; her sister appeared to be in an even worse mood and old granny Walker was the worse for drink and swearing and shouting at her daughter-in-law. 'The sooner I get away from here the better', thought Sylvia as she made her way up the stairs to her room.
"Where do you think you are going? Been out skiving all afternoon; there's dinner to get before Peter gets home so get your 'glad-rags' off and get and do the spuds you lazy bitch. Don't know who is writing to you but there is a letter waiting for you on the hall table."
Sylvia retraced her steps and picking up the envelope returned to the parlour to open it.
"Lady Muck has time to sit in the parlour while muggings does all the work." Complained her sister.

Sylvia opened the envelope and read the enclosed letter a second time before getting up and making her way to her room. She took an old Gladstone bag from on top of the cupboard and then packed in it her meagre wardrobe of clothes and a few treasured possessions; a silver framed photo of her parents with her as a baby and Dora about four year old and her baby bracelet and a locket her mother had given her on her 21st birthday. She hesitated for just a moment taking one last look around the room; they had been such a happy family what had happened to change everything? Most likely it all started with their father's death in the coal-mine; followed shortly after by his wife whom everyone said 'had died from a broken heart'. She called out to Dora that she was leaving but having no response she left the house without a backward glance. She had no intention of walking to the nearest town so using her last few coins she took the bus that would take her away from all the trials and tribulations that she felt living with her sister. 'She can keep the house I am going to make a new life for myself.'

She made her way to the office of Dobson, Dobson and McIntire and soon all was revealed to her. Mrs. Tucker, the old lady she had taken care of for almost ten years had no living relatives and had left everything to Sylvia.
"Well young lady I assume that you understand you are quite a wealthy young woman."
'Young lady,' she thought 'that is a compliment in itself considering I am nearer forty than thirty.'
"I'd like you to continue looking after my inheritance; I

will visit you once a month but at the moment I have very little need for money as I have promised to care for an old lady who lives in Hill House."

Mr. Dobson senior stared at her with what appeared to be a look of amazement. "Did you say Hill House? Have you the right address as I understand the house has been empty for almost twenty years? Gertrude Mitchell was our client and when she died her will stated that her estate be handled by us and used in the upkeep of Hill House but under no circumstances must it be sold. The mystery deepens because only yesterday a stranger entered our office and asked for us to arrange the re-stocking of the small-holding at Hill House with the necessary animals. Chickens, ducks a horse and trap, a few sheep, goats and a cow and the necessary implements that would be required to maintain the land. We thought he had made a mistake when he said that Miss Mitchell had sent him. My brother and I stood by the window to see which direction he took but we missed seeing him leave the office. According to Miss Mitchell's will we must carry out all instructions we receive."

She booked into a hotel and relaxed in the luxury; even if it was only for one night. She didn't sleep well as Mr. Dobson's words kept going over and over in her mind. She tried to reason out the happenings of the last few days. It did seem to be very strange; what had led her to

Hill House? Where had the lady come from? The terrain had been rocky but she hadn't heard her approaching and when she had looked back she had seen about six people standing waving to her; they too seemed to have appeared from no-where. All would be solved on the morrow when she returned to Hill House.

It was a glorious Midsummer's Day; she took the bus to the nearest stop to the lane that led to the mountain and she hoped that she would find her way again to Hill House. As she alighted from the bus she noticed a fragile old man standing close by holding the reins of a horse behind which was a trap.
"Miss Robert's I have been instructed to hand over the reins to you; the horse knows his way to Hill House."
"Can I drop you off anywhere?" She offered as she thought the old man looked about to collapse.
"I have no need of a ride."
She put her bag in the trap and then climbed up and taking the reins the horse needed no encouragement as he trotted off along the lane. As she turned the corner she glanced back but there was no sign of the old man. She recalled Mr. Dobson's words' 'the mystery deepens'. She felt no trepidation as any way of life would be better than the existence she had living with her sister.

Ahead of her was the mountain path, that she had walked so many times, to the next town but it was here that the horse veered to the right and began the uphill climb through a leafy glade; the hot summer sun flickered through the branches it all felt so mystical and magical. She didn't feel alone she felt as though she was being guided to her new home. Hadn't the old lady said that the spirits would guide her home? At the end of the incline the trees thinned out and she found herself on the open mountain-side and there on the top of the hill stood her new home. The front door was open and as she entered the hall-way she was expecting to be greeted by the old lady or one of her friends but there appeared to be no-one about. She called out; "Is there anyone at home?" but received no reply. She left her bag in the hallway and ventured further down the passage; opening a door she entered an immaculate kitchen; although in many ways it was dated but to her eyes it was just perfect. Looking through the window she could see out into the yard where chickens pecked away quite contentedly and a cat lazed in the summer sun. Hearing a dog barking made her realize that she hadn't unharnessed the horse so she quickly retraced her steps. To her amazement the horse was grazing in a field opposite and the trap had been put in the barn. 'Why hadn't anyone answered her?' Weren't they ready to meet her or perhaps they were observing her and summing her up but where was the dear, fragile lady whom she was to care for?

She returned into the house and opened the door into the sitting room; she was mesmerized by its Victorian splendour. The drapes, the furniture, the china in the cabinets and the cosy settee that stood in the bay window. She then entered the room opposite and found it to be a dining room but here she noticed a vast difference everything in the room appeared to take her back to another era to Georgian days. She just couldn't believe her eyes. Feeling in need of respite she returned to the kitchen and was amazed to find the larder well stocked. On her previous visit she hadn't noticed a fire burning in the stove. She quickly filled the kettle and soon it was boiling; she left the tea brewing in the pot and returning to the larder lifted the lid of the bread bin and found a loaf of what appeared to be freshly baked bread and on the shelf under a cloche was a freshly made fruit cake. This was all too perfect. Sitting herself down she began to relax and as she poured the second cup of tea she noticed her lady in the garden. She opened the back door and crossed the yard to where the lady stood petting the cat.

"Hello my dear; I am so glad you have arrived. We want you to make yourself at home and to be happy and please do not be afraid of the spirits they come and go they will never harm you."

"What shall I call you?"

She laughed; a shrill piercing laugh; "When I was young and beautiful everyone called me Gertie; you to may call be Gertie and then I will remain young. I think you might be happy in the bedroom off the sitting room I always found it such a pleasant room and you can leave the bedrooms above for our visitors. Go finish your tea we will talk again soon."

Back in the kitchen Sylvia felt even more bemused; hadn't Mr. Dobson said that Miss Gertrude Mitchell had died some twenty years ago. There was an aura throughout the house but she wasn't afraid. It was a beautiful place and she would make it her home and if the visitors were ghosts so be it. She returned to the sitting room and for the first time noticed the door leading to the room that Miss Gertrude said could be hers. It was delightful; far more up to-date than the other rooms; she could smell the perfume of fresh cut roses and the lace curtains blew gently in the breeze that came through the open French doors; and the late afternoon sun shone on the crystal wind catchers that hung on a rail above the doors. The French doors led out to a beautiful rose garden. Walking along the path and stopping to watch the bees sipping the nectar and covering their bodies with pollen; the butterflies on the purple buddleia and the blackbird singing so sweetly she felt, that for the first time in many a year, she was a peace with the world.

She kept the home ready for 'visitors'; the bedrooms

were kept fresh and the furniture polished and everything spick and span. Occasionally she heard noises in the rooms above but she never encroached on their privacy. She often saw Miss Gertrude walking in the rose garden; and the man that had met her with the horse and trap appeared to be a daily visitor. On a few occasions the lady and gentleman that occasionally occupied the room above hers would venture into the kitchen but it took them almost a year before they spoke to her. They spoke about their time together when they were on the stage. Different 'visitors' came some stopped longer than others; they all appeared to be ancient both in their mode of dress and in age; she often wondered why there were no young 'visitors'.

She stopped by the office of Dobson, Dobson and McIntire once a month and bought a few necessities. Never once did she meet anyone she knew until a spring day about two years later she turned the corner into the High Street and literally bumped into Dora and Peter. Peter was carrying a young child and she immediately noticed Dora's swollen belly.
"Out of our way," Peter pushed her to one side; "A fine sister you turned out to be leaving us in the lurch and not so much as a 'thank you' for all Dora did for you. In the money now are you? Is your house to posh to invite us for a visit?"
"It is not my house; I run a guest house for visitors and

take care of the lady who owns it."

"Liar," shouted Peter, "I hear you bought a grand house in the next valley. I understand it is open house to all the men in the neighbourhood."

She had heard enough and began to walk away from them; "Mean bitch," Peter shouted after her "didn't even give the boy a 'tanner'."

She turned to face her aggressor and opening her purse took a few notes, that she had just received from old Mr. Dobson, and handed them to Dora. "Buy something for the lad and for the baby when it arrives and please don't give any to your old man I think he has enough liquor in his belly to last a life time." She did not wait for any further comment but walked away from them and did not look back.

The following summer; on Midsummer's Day she was sitting on the garden bench outside her back door when she suddenly felt a presence and turning she expected to see one of her usual 'visitors' but instead she saw walking towards her a young man in uniform, As he drew closer she could not take her eyes off the most handsome man she had ever seen. He was not like all her other visitors who were old and grey and wore ancient dress. This man was, as the romantic novels would state, 'tall, dark and handsome'. She knew that he was a 'visitor' as he had appeared, as if out of the blue. He came towards

her and the smile on his face lit up his very countenance.
"May I?" he asked as he pointed to the seat beside her.
"Certainly," she said totally enraptured by his very being.
"Miss Gertrude said that you would welcome me with open arms."
"Just like Miss Gertrude to say that. Have you travelled far?"
"From France where the battle rages and men are dying like flies. Please do not talk about it; my soul has been in torment and I have come here to find a haven with you."

How could she call the presence of Alfred Cooper in her home the love of her life? In the first few months he came and then disappeared for days on end but the closer they became the longer he stayed in his human form not as an apparition that floated in space and time.
"How can I love you," she asked as they sat together in the arbour; "and how can you say you love me? I so hate it when you leave me. Why can't you stay?"
"I do love you but I am a spirit and the only way we can be together for eternity is if you too was one of us and joined us in the spirit world. Since meeting you my soul is no longer in torment; but how I long to journey through time and space with you or stay content in Hill House and open our doors to our friends."

Many weeks passed before she saw him again and the longer they were apart the more she turned his words over and over in her mind. She had nothing to lose; the house on the hill would still be hers to come and go as she wished but she would never, ever be alone again. What had he told her? He had said that if she too was a spirit he could hold her in his arms something that he was unable to do her being human and him a ghost. The more she thought about it the more determined she became to resolve the situation.

It took great courage on her part to put into motion her plan. His visitations were becoming less frequent and she was becoming more and more lonesome without him. In the beginning they spent days and sometimes weeks together but now it was just fleeting moments. She also missed seeing Miss Gertrude and her other 'visitors'. Alfred had told her that if she was one of them they would all be a family together.

It was almost Midsummer and a storm had raged for days and she was due to go to town to visit old Mr. Dobson. She put on her water-proof cape and hitching up the horse to the trap she set off. She decided against continuing her journey when she heard the rumble of thunder; she stopped at the village and posted a letter to Mr. Dobson and then headed back for home. Suddenly, she felt his presence beside her, "I love you" she heard him whisper. "I will never leave you ever again. Miss Gertrude and the family are waiting for you."

She was crossing the bridge over the river when a sudden

flash of lighting scared the horse she felt herself falling and crashing through the wooden structure of the old bridge; then she saw him and felt his arms about her as he broke her fall and then dropped her gently into the pool beneath the waterfall. "I'll be waiting for you my love; come back to us very soon."

She hated being shut in the coffin; she heard the minister's words; "Ashes to ashes; dust to dust...." She felt the weight of the soil as it was thrown on the coffin and then she was free; she left her broken body and soared up to the heavens. Returning to the shrubs that grew near to her grave she heard Peter's words; "well, that's the end of her."

As far as she was concerned it was just the beginning.

1940

The years had been happy for Sylvia and Albert; when they manifested their-selves they spent the time in Hill House and opened their doors to more and more 'visitors' but as apparitions they journeyed the land together watching over the dying and helping them along their journey to peace. On one such journey they saw a poor young woman with two small children sitting in the garden of her bombed out home. They heard her cries for 'help' and taking pity on her they resolved to do something about her terrible situation.

Sylvia took on her human form and visited the solicitors'

office of Dobson, Dobson and McIntire. Mr. McIntire junior was too young to know anything about her so she just walked into his office and asked to see him urgently. She mentioned the Last Will and Testament of the late Miss Sylvia Roberts and handed him a letter saying that the time had now come to carry out Miss Roberts' last wish. She also left with him the address of the young mother. Her job was done she had given Hill House to someone who needed it more than her and her ghostly 'visitors'. The end of the haunting of Hill House was over and no longer would Sylvia and Albert take on their human form but occasionally they would pass by just to check that the family were safe and on one happy day in 1946 they left the house on the hill for-ever as they saw their young woman and her children enfolded in the arms of her soldier husband.

NB:- All peoples' names are fictitious

'Mammy Val's Little Book of Allsorts'

Poetry

Today - By Ella Wheeler Wilcox.

Let me today do something that shall take,
A little sadness from the world's vast store,
And may I be so favoured as to make
Of joys to scanty sum, a little more.

Let me not hurt by any selfish deed,
Or thoughtless word, the heart of foe or friend,
Nor would I pass unseeing worthy need,
Or sin by silence when I should defend.

However meagre be my worldly wealth.
Let me do something that shall aid my kind,
A word of courage, a thought of health,
Dropped as I pass for troubled hearts to find.

Let me tonight look back across the span,
'Twixt dawn and dusk and to my conscience say –
Because of some good act to beast or man
The world is better that I live today.

Note: Many of these poems, it is now hard to believe, were learnt back in 1949, taught to children aged between 9 and 11 years of age in Cwm Pennar Junior School, Mountain Ash. Mr. Idwal Thomas was the headmaster and every Friday afternoon before we were allowed out for an extended play-time we had to learn a poem. These poems, once learnt, were never forgotten by me. Do hope you will find many to please you throughout these pages.

Requiem
By Robert Louis Stevenson

Under the wide and starry sky,
   Dig the grave and let me lie
   Glad did I live and gladly I die,
   And I lay be down with a will.

This is the verse you grave for me,
'Here he lies where he longs to be,
Home is the sailor home from the sea.
And the hunter home from the hills.'

Stevenson wrote this epitaph for his grave many years earlier when he lived in California.

'Mammy Val's Little Book of Allsorts'

Sea Fever
By John Mansfield

I must go down to the sea again, to the lonely sea and the sky,
And all I ask is a tall ship and a star to steer her by,
And a wheels kick and a wind's song and the white sails shaking,
And a grey mist on the sea's face and the grey dawn breaking.

I must go down to the sea again, for the call of the running tide,
Is a wild call and a clear call that may not be denied,
And all I ask is a windy day and the white clouds flying
And a flung spray, and the blown spume, and he seagulls crying.

I must go down to the sea again to the vagrant gypsy life,
To the gull's way and the whale's way where the wind's like a whetted knife,
And all I ask is a merry yarn from a laughing fellow rover,
And a quiet sleep and a sweet dream when the long tricks over.

Time you old Gypsy-man

Time you old gypsy-man,
Will you not stay,
Put up your caravan
Just for one day.

All things I'll give you
Will you be my guest,
Bells for your jennet
Of silver the best.

Goldsmiths shall beat you
A great golden ring,
Peacocks shall bow to you,
Little boys sing.

Oh! And sweet girls
Will festoon you with May
Time you old gypsy
Why hasten away.

Last week in Babylon
Last night in Rome,
Morning, and in the crush
Under Paul's dome.

'Mammy Val's Little Book of Allsorts'

Under Paul's dial
You tighten your rein –
Only a moment
And off once again.

Off to some city
Now blind in the womb,
Off to another.
Ere that's in the tomb.

Time you old gypsy
Will you not stay
Put up your caravan
Just for one day.

By Ralph Hodgson

O! Many a shaft, at random sent,
Finds, mark the archer little meant,
And many a word at random spoken,
May soothe or wound a heart that's broken

By Sir Walter Scott.

Upon Westminster Bridge
By William Wordsworth

Earth has not anything to show more fair,
Dull would he be of soul who could pass by
A sight so touching in its majesty,
This city now, doth, like a garment wear
The beauty of the morning, silent, bare
Ships, towers, domes, theatres and temples lie
Open unto the fields and to the sky,
All bright and glistening in the smokeless air,
Never, did sun more beautifully steep
In his first splendour, valley, rock or hill,
Ne'er saw I, never felt a calm so deep,
The river glideth on its own sweet will,
Dear God! The very houses seem asleep
And all that mighty heart is lying still.

Creeds
By Ella Wheeler Wilcox

So many Gods so many creeds
So many paths that wind and wind
While just the art of being kind
Is all this sad world needs.

The Reaper
By William Wordsworth

Behold her, single in the field,
Yon solitary Highland Lass!
Reaping and singing by herself;
Stop here, or gently pass!
Alone she cuts and binds the grain,
And sings a melancholy strain
O listen! For the vale profound
Is overflowing with the sound.

No nightingale did ever chaunt
More welcome notes to weary bands

Of travellers in some shady haunt
    Among Arabian sands:
A voice so thrilling ne'er was heard
In spring-time from the cuckoo-bird,
    Breaking the silence of the seas
    Among the furthest Hebrides.

Will no-one tell me what she sings?
Perhaps the plaintive number flow
For old, unhappy, far-off things,
    And battles long ago:
Or is it some more humble lay,
    Familiar matter of today?
Some natural sorrow, loss or pain
That has been and may be again?

What'er the theme, the maiden sang
As if her song could have no ending;
    I saw her singing at her work,
    And o'er her sickle bending;
    I listen'd motionless and still
    And as I mounted up the hill,
    The music in my heart I bore,
Long after it was heard no more.

Elegy

Written in a Country Church-yard

By Thomas Gray

The curfew tolls the knell of parting day,
The lowing herd winds slowly o'er the lea,
The ploughman homeward plods his weary way,
And leaves the world to darkness and to me.

Now fades the glimmering landscape on the sight,
And all the air a solemn stillness holds,
Save where the beetle wheels his droning flight
And drowsy tinklings lull the distant folds.

Save now from yonder ivy-mantled tower
The moping owl does to the moon complain
Of such a, wandering near her secret bower,
Molest her ancient solitary reign.

Beneath those rugged elms, the yew-tree's shade,
Where heaves the turf in many a mouldering heap,
   Each in his narrow cell for ever laid,
   The rude Forefathers of the hamlet sleep.

The breezy call of incense-breathing morn,
The swallow twittering from the straw built shed,
   The cock's shrill clarion, or the echoing horn,
   No more shall rouse them from their lowly bed.

For them no more the blazing hearth shall burn,
   Or busy housewife ply her evening care:
   No children run to lisp their sire's return,
   Or climb the knees the envied kiss to share.

   Oft did the harvest to the sickle yield,
Their farrow oft the stubborn glebe has broken;
   How jocund did they drive their team afield!
How bow'd the woods beneath their sturdy stroke

   Let not Ambition mock their useful toil,
   Their homely joys and destiny obscure:
   Nor Grandeur hear with a disdainful smile
   The short and distant annals of the Poor.

   The boast of heraldry, the pomp of power,
   And all that beauty, all that wealth e'er gave,

'Mammy Val's Little Book of Allsorts'

Awaits alike the inevitable hour:-
The paths of glory lead but to the grave.

Nor you, ye Proud, impute to these the fault
If Memory 'er their tomb no trophies raise,
Where through the long-drawn aisle the fretted vault
The pealing anthem swells the note of praise.
Can storied urn or animated bust
Back to its mansion call the fleeting breath?
Can Honour's voice provoke the silent dust,
Or Flattery soothe the dull cold ear of Death?

Perhaps in this neglected spot is laid
Some heart once pregnant with celestial fire;
Hands, that the rod of empire might have sway'd,
Or waked to ecstasy the living lyre:

But Knowledge to their eyes her ample page,
Rich with the spoils of time, did ne'er enroll,
Chill Penury repress'd their noble rage,
And froze the genial current of the soul.

Full many a gem of purest ray serene
The dark unfathom'd caves of ocean bear;
Full many a flower is born to blush unseen,
And waste its sweetness on the desert air.

Some village-Hampden, that with dauntless breast

The little tyrant of his fields withstood,
Some mute inglorious Milton here may rest,
Some Cromwell, guiltless of his country's blood.

Th' applause of list'ning senates to command,
The threats of pain and ruin to despise,
To scatter plenty o'er a smiling land,
And read their history in a nation's eyes.
Their lot forbad: no circumscribed alone
Their growing virtues, but their crimes confined,
Forbad to wade through slaughter to a throne,
And shut the gates of mercy on mankind,

The struggling pangs of conscious truth to hide,
To quench the blushes of ingenuous shame,
Or heap the shrine of Luxury and Pride
With incense kindled at the Muse's flame.

Far from the madding crowd's ignoble strife
Their sober wishes never learn'd to stray;
Along the cool sequester'd vale of life
They kept the noiseless tenour of their way.

Yet e'en these bones from insult to protect
Some frail memorial still erected nigh,
With uncouth rhymes and shapeless sculpture deck'd,
Implores the passing tribute of a sigh.

Their name, their years, spelt by th' unletter'd Muse,
   The place of fame and elegy supply:
And many a holy text around she strews,
   That teach the rustic moralist to die.

For who, to dumb forgetfulness a prey,
   This pleasing anxious being o'er resign'd
Left the warm precincts of the cheerful day,
   Nor cast one longing look behind?
On some fond breast the parting soul relies,
   Some pious drops the closing eye requires;
E'en from the tomb the voice of Nature cries,
   E'en in our ashes live their wonted fire.

For thee, who, mindful of th' unhonour'd dead,
   Dost in these lines their artless tale relate;
If chance, by lonely contemplation led,
   Some kindred spirit shall inquire thy fate;-

Haply some hoary-headed swain may say,
   Oft have we seen him at the peep of dawn
Brushing with hasty steps the dews away,
   To meet the sun upon the upland lawn;

'There at the foot of yonder nodding beech
   That wreathes its old fantastic roots so high.
His listless length at noontide would he stretch,

And pore upon the brook that babbles by.

'Hard by you wood, now smiling as in scorn,
Muttering his wayward fancies he would rove;
Now drooping, woeful wan, like one forlorn,
Or crazed with care, or cross'd in hopeless love.

'One morn I miss'd him on the custom'd hill
Along the heath, and near his favourite tree;
Another came; nor yet beside the rill,
Nor up the lawn, nor at the wood was he;
'The next with dirges due in sad array
Slow through the church-way path we saw him borne,-
Approach and read (for thou canst read) the lay
Graved on the stone beneath you aged thorn.'

The Epitaph
Here rests his head upon the lap of Earth
A youth to Fortune and to Fame unknown,
Fair Science frown'd not on his humble birth,
And Melacholy marked him for her own.

Large was his bounty, and his soul sincere,
Heaven did a recompense as largely send;
He gave to Misery all he had, a tear,

He gained from Heaven ('twas all he wish'd) a friend.

No farther seek his merits to disclose,
Or draw his frailities from their dread abode
(There they alike in trembling hope repose),
The bosom of his Father and his God.

Thomas Gray (1716-1771)

Note: As this book is for adults I have printed the complete poem but will point out that all we learnt at school was the first two verses and the verse 'Full many a gem of purest ray serene....'but was instructed to read the complete poem.

A Few Native American Sayings:-

May the stars carry your sadness away;
May the flower fill your heart with beauty;
May hope forever wipe away your tears;
And above all; May silence make you strong.
Chief Dan George

"Behold, my friends, the spring is come;
The earth has gladly received the embraces of the sun
And we shall soon see the results of their love!"
Sitting Bull

Every Indian outbreak that I have ever known has resulted from broken promises and broken treaties by the Government.
Buffalo Bill (Cody)

A promise must never be broken.
Alexander Hamilton

Apache Blessing

May the sun bring you new energy by day;
May the moon softly restore you by night;
May the rain wash away your worries;
May the breeze blow his strength into your being;
May you walk gaily through the world
And know its beauties all the days of your life.

The Song of Hiawatha
By Henry W. Longfellow

Note: I have just given you a 'taste' of one of the most delightful story/poems I believe has ever been written. Form your own opinion and read the whole fantastic work by Henry Longfellow.

The Peace Pipe:

'O my children! My poor children!
Listen to the words of wisdom,
Listen to the words of warning,
From the lips of the Great Spirit,
From the master of Life, who made you!

"I have given you lands to hunt in,
I have given you streams to fish in,
I have given you bear and bison,
I have given you roe and reindeer,
I have given you brant[1] and beaver,
Filled the marshes full of wild-fowl,
Filled the rivers full of fishes;
Why then are you not contented?
Why then will you hunt each other?

"I am weary of your quarrels,
Weary of your wars and bloodshed,
Weary of your prayers for vengeance,
Of your wranglings and disssensions;
All your strength is in your union,
All your danger is in discord;
Therefore be at peace henceforward,
And as brothers live together.

"I will send a Prophet to you,
A Deliverer of the nations,
Who shall guide you and shall teach you,
Who shall toil and suffer with you.
If you listen to his counsels,
You will multiply and prosper;
If the warnings pass unheeded,
You will fade away and perish!

Note:- 1 Brant – a wild goose.

'Mammy Val's Little Book of Allsorts'

Me and my 'Big-foot'

News Headlines 18th December 1970

In bad weather conditions a Cessna 421 crashed in Mohican Memorial State Forest.

No survivors – pilot and seven passengers killed instantly.

21st December – There appears to be a mystery with regards to the number of passengers on board the Cessna 421 charter plane; it has been confirmed that there were eight passengers. The body of Lady Annabel Richardson has not been found. An intensive search of the area revealed no clues and the search had to be called off as weather conditions became critical.

New York July 2000

I paused out-side the book-shop in Manhattan and gazed

admiringly into the window. The window had a vast display of my first book that was already receiving rave reviews; was it fact or was it fiction? This was the question every-one was asking. Just the one word title of the book was enough to stir the imagination of the general public; *'Takuhe'* the Sioux word for the Sasquatch and as the author I was just entering the shop for an arranged book-signing. Up until this very moment I had kept out of the lime-light and as far as everyone was concerned I was just a mature lady with a vivid imagination who had written a 'best seller'. The nom-de-plume on the cover was Lizzy England. I hadn't been inside a beauty parlour since 1970 and here I was dressed in an elegant suit and my make-up and hair done to perfection. Looking at myself in a mirror I could not recognize the image that looked back at me.

My story begins:

I have little memory of that fateful day back in December 1970. I can recall that I was relieved to have found a charter flight that would take me from Charleston to Lake Michigan to spend Christmas with friends. A broken romance had left me devastated; I had been so deeply in love with Justin Denison and had arranged a great Christmas just for the two of us when I had hoped he would propose to me. He was everything a girl would desire in a man; so handsome; a top job and a flash car; I ignored the fact that he always appeared to be without money and believe me when I say I was only too eager to give him 'hand-outs' and on many occasions paid the bills but what did I care I had plenty of money to spend; I was what my friends would say 'rolling in it.'

I had left England back in '66 after the untimely death of my parents. For a few years I had led a reclusive life until I met Justin and as I just said I fell immediately in love with him. He was so charming and caring and made me feel so very special; especially in bed when he took me to the waters of Lethe. We drank champagne for breakfast and would return to bed for more love-making. No lover had ever taken me to such heights. The flight I took on that day was to get away from Charleston and the memory of how I had been betrayed. Looking back I suppose I had a lucky break when I found that he was practically living with another woman and had no top job and had been living off me as he knew how wealthy I was. I made up my mind there and then that in no way would I enter into another relationship and disclose who I was or my financial situation even if it meant changing my name. I had already made up my mind that in the New Year I would return to England.

Many flights had been cancelled but as the pilot and fellow passengers were all eager to get home for

Christmas we took off. I remember that we were told to fasten our safety belts as the pilot was expecting some turbulence. I noticed that visibility was almost zero as the light snow fall had now turned into a blizzard. 'Soon clear' said the pilot, 'once we are over the forest'. Was it the fact that I hadn't been able to fasten my seat belt that saved my life?

I recall a feeling of feeling so very cold; even my faux fur coat didn't keep out the icy blast. I wanted to sleep but something in the back of my mind kept telling me 'don't go to sleep'. I focused my mind on the pain I felt in every part of my body and when it was almost getting to hard to bear I felt myself being lifted up and strong arms holding me close; then it was oblivion. How long had I been unconscious? I no longer felt cold; I felt as though I was encased in a cocoon of soft fleecy blankets. I slowly opened by eyes and tried to focus on the dimly lit surrounding; some-one was holding my hand; was I in hospital? Was it a doctor or a nurse checking my pulse; I turned my head and saw an animal's paw holding my hand; I must have fainted and when I came to a kindly voice was saying 'don't be afraid; I will not harm you I saved your life and brought you to my cabin'.

I sipped the drink I was offered and looked into two soft brown eyes that were too human to be those of an animal. My first thought had been that I had been taken to the den of a 'Big-foot' but this was no den it was a log cabin and a roaring fire burned brightly in the hearth.

The man, for that is what he was, was way above average height and the hair on his head was long and dark and his face was almost fully covered in hair except for his mouth, nose and eyes; his hands were as hairy as his face. He was clothed, in what appeared to be, a hand-made leather jerkin worn over a home-spun check shirt and his trousers were of a course fabric.

'Welcome to Christmas', he said putting his arm around my shoulders helping me to raise myself up. 'I am glad to say I found no broken bones only you have received some very bad bruising and I have dressed your wounds.'

'Christmas' I murmured; 'is it really Christmas?' I couldn't take my eyes off the 'monster' that stood before me but my mind was saying 'this is no monster; he must be human'. Every movement I tried to make caused me great pain and after he had fed me some type of porridge I was glad to lie back down and must have soon fallen asleep. How many days this continued I cannot recollect but it was well into the New Year before I became lucid. Again I began to wonder where was I. Surely I must now be in hospital as I appeared to be on a drip and could also feel a catheter tube attached to me. Opening my eyes I could see I was in the same room and suddenly I began to feel afraid; what was happening to me?

'Hello Annabel; you have been very poorly but I am glad

to say you are now on the road to recovery. You have had pneumonia; please don't look so scared I am a qualified doctor and care for a lot of the people in the nearby town. When you are fully recovered I will tell you more.'

'How do you know my name?'

'When I found you I also found your attaché case and purse. The purse was in your hand but I found your case on the plane; sadly there was nothing I could do for any of the passengers. Your case remains locked but I checked your purse for your identity. Do not concern yourself about things at the moment you need to get strong. The ladies from the town have made some nourishing broth for you.' He lifted me up with one arm and placed another soft down pillow behind my head. How could I be afraid of such a kind man? I let him feed me spoonful after spoonful of the delicious broth. Left alone I no longer felt like sleep and now sitting up in bed I could see around the room; it was void of clutter and all the furniture appeared to be hand-made. The bedspread on the bed was of a patchwork design and obviously hand-crafted. Then I became aware that I had on a cotton shift void of buttons or any elaborate embroidery. Who had undressed me and who had been caring for me?

It wasn't until the next day that I saw my 'nurses' and there was no mistaking that they were from an Amish society. They greeted me warmly but said very little as they set about washing me and changing the dressings on the wounds on my legs and arms. 'You must thank God that the doctor saved your life' said the one named Sara. 'When you are well you may visit us and we will pray together; our prayers have been answered that you have recovered.' They visited twice a day different ladies from the Amish township; some were chattier and I soon learned that the doctor's cabin was in Mohican Memorial State Forest and they were from one of the communities in Holmes County.

Slowly I got to know the doctor and as my health improved he spent more time with me. Evenings were the nicest part when we sat together by a roaring fire whilst the wind roared outside and snow drifts formed high around the cabin. One evening he related to me the reason why he had become a recluse.

'I was at the end of my final year as an intern; after the summer vacation with my friends I would be taking up a practice in the local hospital. I had worked hard and played hard and now I would practice the fruits of my labour I would be a qualified doctor. How good it sounded; Daniel Benson M.D. The summer vacation was marred when I began to feel ill; I was hospitalized; tests were done but nothing adverse materialized so I was sent home with the suggestion that I took a quiet vacation to recover fully before taking up my appointment. I decided that I would like to visit the Mohican Memorial Forest so

I rented a cabin; not this secluded one. I spent my days hiking and fishing but although I no longer felt ill I was becoming stressed when I became aware that a morning shave wasn't sufficient; the more I shaved the more hair seemed to grow and then I began to notice the hair on my arms and legs and body hair was daily growing thicker. I gave up shaving and on a visit into town I went to the library and diagnosed my condition; with the medical knowledge that I had it appeared I was suffering from hypertricosis; excess hair growth. I knew there was no cure so it was then I bought this cabin and for quite a while lived as a hermit; living off the land and the wild life. On a few occasion as I wandered the paths of the forest I was chased by my fellow man shouting 'I saw a Sasquatch'. They never took time to note that I wore clothes. Head-lines soon appeared in local papers saying that a 'Big-foot' had been sighted in the forest. Okay I must admit I must look like a hairy monster but according to legend they are of high stature. I am tall but my six foot six inches and size 12 shoes don't make me a Sasquatch.

An epidemic in one of the local Amish communities brought me out of hibernation; so to speak and I went to their aid. I became friendly with the community and they in turn assisted me. They did not treat me as a 'freak'; as this is what I felt I was. I do not venture far from the forest but if needed, at any time, I usually travel to them late evening or when they come and fetch me. It is no life but I am content; I work long hours doing research and perhaps one day some-one will publish my volumes. Now may I ask why you show no fear of me and why now when you are free to go you remain?'

'In a different way, I too am glad to 'hide away' I have been hurt by my friends who class me as 'Miss Moneybags'; I want to be loved for myself not for my money.'

'All your friends or just one particular one?' he questioned.

'The man I loved and thought would marry me.'

'You should return to civilization not all men are the same; 'Mr. Right' is out there waiting for you.'

I could see the tender look in his eyes and I wanted to put my arms around him; he was as human as myself surely he needed to be loved.

The thaw had set in and still I remained with Dan; we talked and his knowledge of flora and fauna he passed on to me. The ladies from the Amish community brought me clothes and requested that I visit them. Who now would recognize me as Lady Annabel Richardson? In my appearance I was now an Amish lady. My dresses were hand-made of blue or green cotton; I had also been given white aprons and head-scarves. These I only wore when I visited our friends. Mostly I walked around 'our home' barefooted and walking further afield I wore soft moccasin type slippers. How can I explain why I now felt so happy and contented?

There were times when Dan took himself off into the forest and I didn't see him for days; I really missed him and was so glad when he safely returned. There was no getting away from the fact that he liked his reclusive life but as the weeks went by we grew closer; I noticed a look of anguish upon his face when I teased him; to me, beneath the growth of hair, was a kind, loving man; he really must have been so handsome.
'Why do you spend so much time hiking in the forest?' I questioned him as we sat outside in the beautiful spring evening. The birds were singing and if one sat quietly one could hear the forest animals 'talking' to each other.
He hesitated a while before replying; 'Why do you think?'
I just looked at him and shook my head; 'I have no idea; surely you know this forest like the back of your hand; what more knowledge are you seeking?'
He rose from his seat and began to walk down the path towards the lake. 'Where are you going?' I called after him and hurried along the path to join him. I looked up into his sad, brown eyes and could see that his eyes were filled with tears. I put my hand on his arm to offer him comfort for whatever was troubling him.
'Annabel, are you really unaware of why I go off for days on end; don't you realize what is bothering me? I

may look like a big hairy monster but underneath all this camouflage I am a man; a man with a man's needs. Having you so close and not being able to take you in my arms for fear of rejection and not being able to tell you that 'I love you' is so painful.'

'Wasn't that easy Dan? You just said those three little words; and I was so pleased to hear them. To me you are not a 'monster'; a name by which you referred yourself to; you are a man and I too have fallen in love with you. Please do not hide yourself away from me.'

'How can you possibly love me?' He put his big hairy arms around me and pulled me close; I nestled into his hairy chest; for the first time in many a year I felt safe.

From that moment we became a couple; each evening, as the sun was beginning to set we walked together through the forest; sometimes even staying out all night in a deserted cave. It might have been a little dishonest of us but we had our secret places where we could 'spy' on the campers in the park. After spending the night away from the cabin we would spend most of the day in bed. I loved the feel of his hands upon my naked body; his kisses and caresses were passionate but to my disappointment the ultimate act of love never took place. My body burned for him and I know that he too wanted to make our relationship complete.

The summer came early and I offered my help to our friends the Amish. The one called Sara, who had cared for me after the crash, took me to one-side. 'Annabel, we are pleased for you that you have found happiness but it is not good for you to go on living with the doctor; you must come and live with us and take lessons to be a good wife and when you are ready then we will arrange your wedding and it is then and only then that you can be with the man you love as your husband.'

I returned home; tired after a day's hard work, and was disappointed to find that Dan wasn't at home. I needed to be comforted as Sara's words were churning over and over in my stomach; how could Dan and I ever marry? Dan hadn't gone 'walk-about' for some-time so I began to think that as the evening was so hot he might have gone for a swim. Putting my sandals back on I strolled down the path towards the lake and there in the twilight I could see him in the water. He looked like a big brown bear; I sat and watched my heart filled with love for him. He strode out of the water he shook himself just like a big English sheep dog would have done and then he saw me.
'Coming for a swim?' he called to me.
'Haven't brought my bathers,' I replied.
'Who needs bathers? Only the man in the moon is watching us.'
I slipped off my cotton shift and was tempted to leave on

my bra and pants; but he shouted 'You don't need to leave them on.' I ran through the long grass completely naked; excitement was making my temperature rise. I ran into his arms and picking me up he walked back into the water. He was standing in the shallow water's edge; the water was gently lapping against his thighs and still he held me in his arms; I felt his moist lips upon mine; 'my little water nymph', he said and gently dropped me into the water. I swam away from him out into the centre of the lake and suddenly he appeared beneath me; he pulled me towards him and began kissing me. 'Race you to the shore,' he said as he moved away from me.

By the time I reached the water's edge Dan was already waiting for me; was this going to be the coming together of two rivers; would we at last me united and be as one. The moon shone, as bright as day, and I could see that he was ready for me and was quite surprised to see that his manhood was void of hair. I was blind to his hairy body all I could see was a handsome man who was ready for love.

He pulled me down in the long grass and for a while I felt that he was not going to make love to me. The fore-play took me to hidden heights and I cried out in ecstasy time and time again. We both laughed when an owl screeched back as if replying to my mating call. I heard the words that I had so longed to hear; 'I love you my little water nymph; I cannot put off the inevitable I have wanted to make love to you from that first evening when we sat by the fire together but I am afraid of the consequences what if you become pregnant and one day our son will become like me?' The moment to make love was lost.

'I love you Dan; so what if I do become pregnant? You have an illness of which the cases registered are few and far between. Sara told me today that I should go and live with them and take lessons and then when the time is right she wants us to be married; she more or less implied we were living in sin. Well, if that is the case we may as well be more sinful.' I moved closer to him and instead of him taking me to hidden heights the tables were turned.

'No more, no more you are tormenting me you little minx;' he pulled me astride him and I screamed out in pleasure as he entered me. I had waited for this moment and was in heaven he was a perfect lover. We rolled together in the long grass and swam in the lake and time and time again made love until the moon left the heavens and the sun began to rise in the eastern sky.

Our door was always open to visits from the Amish in the nearby town but on our return we turned the key in the door and after eating an appetizing breakfast of cereal and fruit we retired to our bed and made up for lost time.

That evening as we sat out on the deck Dan turned to me with a huge grin on his face; 'by the way, if I recall rightly, you proposed to me last night. I think we had better pay Sara a visit and see what she suggests about us getting married.'

It was November, almost a year had elapsed since Dan had rescued me from the plane crash, that we were married. We had both agreed to all the Amish conditions; even to me living with Sara for the last month before our wedding. The snow lay deep and crisp upon the ground and the moon shone brightly down upon me as I entered the old church. I was amused to see Dan waiting for me; somehow or other they had found a dark suit for him; again, I assumed the handy-work of the women of the town. The township had, because of their love for the doctor, agreed that our wedding should take place at dusk. It was usual for Amish weddings that invitations be sent out to distant towns but as Sara had agreed our wedding was different and only her close family and those that knew Dan were invited. Sara had made my dress; it was plain but beautiful and her needlework was exceptional and my veil was like gossamer crocheted by one of the senior ladies of the township. The women and girls were all dressed in their Sunday best dresses of green or blue their aprons spotless white as were their little caps or headscarves. The men, also wore their plain dark Sunday best clothes and wide brim hats. We took our vows, beneath an arch of ribbons, in the wooden church where in the front pews sat the elders of the town. Where had they found all the food for our wedding 'breakfast'? On the trestle tables taking pride of place were jugs of celery; I smiled to myself when I recalled weddings I had been to when the church and tables had been festooned with flowers; celery was certainly different; I had heard that this was a custom with the Amish in Holmes County as it was the last crop of the season.

It was almost dawn before we travelled back to the cabin in a borrowed horse and trap. Dan picked me up and carried me into our home. 'How romantic,' I said; 'carrying me over the threshold'.
'Well, Mrs. Benson you have just promised to 'honour and obey me', so get your wedding finery off and let us go and have some fun.'
We certainly made up for the month we had been apart; we ignored the tapping on the door as someone came to fetch the horse and trap; we needed no nourishment, our love making was food enough for us. We took each other to paradise; and there in the garden of Eden we were the only two in the world; our cries of ecstasy were carried on the wind that howled like a pack of wolves around our cabin but we were oblivious to the out-side world. We were complete; we were united in love.

Spring came and then summer and Dan knew how disappointed I was that with each month that passed I still hadn't conceived. It was the beginning of Fall; the leaves on the maple trees had turned yellow but as the autumn sun shone through the forest they sparkled as if they had been turned to gold.

'Let us take a break and go up into the mountains;' suggested Dan, 'I know just the place where we can be alone it might be the only chance we'll get before winter sets in.'

I visited Sara and told her not to worry about us as we were taking a break for a few days.

'God go with you my child; perhaps come next summer I will be holding your baby in my arms; my blessings go with you.'

I kept Sara's words close to my heart as we started our journey late that evening and journeyed on throughout the night through thick forest, open meadows and then to the high peaks of the mountains. I was amazed at how he could find his way but guessed that it was a route he had taken many a time. It was early morning and an autumnal sun was just beginning to show its face when exhausted after the long trek we came across a dilapidated cabin in a clearing. We were really in the wilderness, surely no-one would come this way.

'This is mine,' Dan said, 'I built it quite a while ago; not a very good job I must admit.'

The door creaked on its unoiled hinges as Dan opened it. 'Would madam like to be carried over the threshold?'

'I am exhausted; you can carry me wherever you like.'
'Then it will be bed for both of us; we shall sleep until night-fall and then we shall have fun and games.'
I laughed as the bed creaked and groaned under our weight; I was waiting for it to collapse. Dan kissed me gently and then taking me in his arms we fell asleep. I woke up before Dan; his arms were still tightly around me and as I tried to move he pulled me back; 'Where do you think you are going?'
'Just to find something to eat; I forgot what you packed.'
Dan soon got the smoky old stove lit and soon we dined on hot coffee and some of Sara's flavoursome homemade bread and sausages. 'It is snowing', I said to Dan as I peered out of the grimey window. 'What if we have to stay here all the winter?'
'Too early for a heavy fall; it will be gone by morning. Now you have had your fill I need my desert.' Dan jested. 'I promised you fun and games so to start get your clothes off.'
'I will be cold; it is freezing I don't wish to leave the stove.'
'I will soon warm you up;' he started by removing my woolen coat and then lifting up my dress he pulled it over my head. Then picking me up he carried me to the bed; I watched by the glow of the stove and the oil lamp that flickered on the table as he removed his clothes. Naked as the day that he was born he jumped into bed beside me; I felt the bed give way and was waiting for it to

collapse but it stayed firm beneath us as he searched for me underneath the animal skin covering. The only way I can describe the feel of his hands upon my naked body was like being smoothed by a fur glove; he soon had me in raptures as he teased and tormented me; I tried to pull him to me I wanted him so desperately but he continued touching me and making me cry out in passion; exhausted from the fore-play I fell asleep in his arms only to wake up to find him flaccid inside me and fast asleep. Surely he hadn't made love to me while I had slept. Had I been that exhausted not to have felt his love making? It was pay-back time; I began to tease him and as soon as I had him emotionally roused he was awake and more than ready for love making.

We spent three rapturous days in the old cabin and it is a wonder that the old wooden framed bed hadn't collapsed as we romped and rolled upon it. On the trek home I felt quite mystical, for lack of a better word, was it a foresight or just a woman's intuition that I had conceived Dan's baby.
'Happy New Year Darling,' I greeted Dan on the first morning of a new year; 'I have a special present for you. I wanted to give it to you for Christmas but thought it best to keep it until the New Year.'
'What have you hidden from me?'
'A baby,' I said patting my stomach. 'Come the middle

of June you will be a daddy.'
He took me in his arms; 'I knew it would work away from here my old cabin has magical powers.' He teased.
'I don't think it was the cabin that had magical powers but the amorous lover that I was with. Are you pleased?'
'You know I am my darling it is just…'
I put my hand up to his mouth. 'Don't say it and please don't even think it. Baby will be just perfect.'

For the last few weeks before my due date Sara insisted I stayed with her; she mothered me like a mother hen mothers her chicks. 'You will fetch Dan when the contractions start; I want him here with me.' Sara made her promise and I knew she would not break it. Did baby know that its father only ventured into town as night fell? A brilliant moon shone in through the un-curtained window or the room where I lay. I had paced the room for what seemed hours but now Sara told me to take to my bed. 'Not until Dan arrives, baby can't be born until Dan is here.'
'He is on his way;' Sara said as she examined me. There appeared to be no end to this lovely woman's talents. 'So is baby.'
'No, no'. I screamed as I was gripped by the worse of all the pains.
'Who is making all this noise,' said the voice of my husband. He took my hand as Sara told me that with the next contraction baby's head would be visible. The

feeling of his soft hand upon my head took away all my pain and with the next push our son was born.

'Welcome Samuel Daniel Benson' said Dan 'and who has been a clever girl?' Sara left us to our moment of elation. Age had never mattered to me but I had turned thirty the previous year and it was heart-breaking to feel that I would never be a mother and what joy I now felt as I held our son to my breast. He was perfect in every way and the joy that Dan felt radiated from his eyes. Yet, I also felt the hidden pain at the words he never spoke but were always on his mind.

Sam was a delight to us, his doting parents, and by the time he was three year old Dan would take him fishing and hiking in the woods. The little one knew more about the wild-life in the forest than children years older. He never questioned his father's appearance. It was coming up to Sam's fifth birthday and I began to notice a daily change in Dan; he had the previous March celebrated his forty-fifth birthday and since that time I noticed that his brown hair was turning quickly grey; over the ensuing months our love-making had become non-existent. He worked long hours at his desk; when I questioned him his reply had been 'that he was putting his papers in order'.

'Why is daddy so hairy,' asked young Sam a few days before his birthday.

'The Amish like to grow long beards and don't like to cut

their hair.' Sam appeared content with my reply. As I turned to continue my chores I noticed Dan disappearing into his room; had he heard Sam's question? The thought bothered me.

'I am going for a walk,' said Dan as I settled Sam down for the night. He kissed his son and then gave me a hug; 'I love you so much Annabel, always remember that.'

I remained awake all night and by the morning I had a deep feeling of ill-boding that something was wrong. Why hadn't Dan returned?

I quickly got Sam dressed and walked the mile to Sara's home.

'Don't worry yourself he will return,' but her words did not lighten the load upon my heart and in her eyes I could see that she too was concerned. Two days elapsed and still Dan hadn't returned.

The elders of the village gathered together and decided they would elect a group of young men to go and look for Dan. 'I believe I know where he has gone; he took me there when we had a few days break away from home.' I couldn't tell them the route but somehow in my mind I felt I could lead them there but how? We had travelled by moon-light everything would look different in the day-light.

Leaving Sam with Sara, his birthday forgotten, I went with the men to search for Dan. Closing my eyes I remembered hearing a water fall; I remembered crossing a bridge that led to a fertile valley and from there the mountain trail that took us high above the timber line and then down again to another valley and there in the small clearing by a lake we would find Dan's cabin. We found the clearing but to my dismay all that remained of the cabin was burnt out timbers. I went to rush forward but one of the young men held me back. I collapsed in his arms when I heard that they had found Dan's body; all they said was that it appeared that Dan must have been asleep when the oil lamp had tipped over and as the cabin was old and the timbers rotten it would have soon be set ablaze.

How they got me back to the town is lost in my memory; the young man whose arms I had collapsed in, I was later told, had carried me for quite a way before letting others help me along the route. They later brought Dan's remains back and buried him in their cemetery. I returned to the cabin to pick up my few treasured possessions and Dan's files of his research papers and went to live with Sara. I know turned to the Amish more and more; their quiet way of life was a comfort to me. Thankfully Sam was a happy little boy and grew in stature and matured very quickly and was a highly intelligent little boy. In my mind I hoped that he would one day fulfil the dream that his father had but never accomplished.

My story does not end there; at the time of Dan's death a cloud hung over me for quite some-time; had he, like many an animal, gone away to find a place to die; did he know that he had not long to live and wanted to take that pain away from me; one other thought was that he had heard Sam's question and didn't wish for the child to face what his father was; had he arranged his own death? The answer to that I would never know. One thing I did know was that I loved him and he loved me and from that love Sam was conceived. I vowed then that I would never marry again.

Some years later that vow was broken; it took me some time to realize that I was getting very fond of Jacob Miller; we met at social gatherings and as is the custom he asked Sara's permission to court me; this went before the elders and within a month our marriage was arranged. Our wedding day came after the harvest and it was a grand occasion. Sam loved Jacob and learnt so much from him. By the time I was forty-five we had three more children, all daughters. Jacob delighted in our family.

Sam has left the Amish community; he has achieved my dream for him and soon will become the doctor his father wanted to be, I gave him Dan's research paper's on his 21st birthday. We are still very close and it was his idea for me to write his father's story. Our lovely daughter's will soon be looking to lead their own lives. It will be

hard for Jacob to part with his 'girls' but I tell him that the day will come when we will be grand-parents and that happy times will continue.
Jacob had been a loving, wonderful husband and went along with Sam's suggestion to write Dan's story; he supported me in every way.

As for Lady Annabel Richardson; had she disappeared off the face of the earth; well, not quite I had kept in touch with my solicitor from the moment I was fully recovered. I had made him promise not to reveal to anyone my whereabouts. Spending very little over the years my money had accumulated; a generous amount had been turned over to Sam on his 21st birthday and the rest is there for a 'rainy day'.

Now standing outside the book shop in Manhattan I am in a dilemma; when I enter the shop shall I just remain the author 'Lizzie England' or reveal that I am Annabel Miller from an Amish community in Ohio or reveal to the world that I am the lady in the story; a story that is fact not fiction and I am Lady Annabel Richardson. What is the old saying? 'The truth will out'.
Lights flashed as I stepped into the book-shop; I wasn't aware that the press would be waiting for me.
'Have we been correctly informed that you are Lady Annabel Richardson?' Was the first question I was asked.

'Who told you that?' I said in almost a whisper.
'Well, is it true? Our source says that it is a name you used as a child when you played a game of 'make believe'.
Surely an old grudge couldn't last that long? My best friend Diane had fallen out with me when one of our group of boy-friends had chosen to take me out when Diane had been longing for him to pick her. She was the only one that knew my 'pen-name'.
So, at last the truth was out. More questions that I refused to answer and politely I stated that I was there for a 'book-signing' not an interrogation. How I longed to get away; I hated this back-biting, dog eat dog world that I had left in 1970.

I spent the night in the five star hotel and the next morning immediately after breakfast I hired a cab to take me to the station. It would have been so much quicker and easier to have flown back to Ohio but no way would I ever get on a plane. As the train neared my destination I went to the 'ladies' and taking from my over-night bag my cotton dress and little white cap and apron I quickly changed. I neatly folded my fancy clothes; knowing that I would need something suitable for Sam's graduation I slipped my feet back into my mules. For the time being Lady Annabel Richardson would remain hidden away. I couldn't wait to return to my husband and family.
As I walked through the terminus; everywhere I looked I

could see my picture and the head-lines 'Lady Annabel Richardson returns from the dead; is she the lady in the story that lived with a 'Big-foot'? No-one looked towards the shy, unassuming woman, dressed in the mode of an Amish lady as I made my way to the horse and trap where my husband, dressed in black and wearing a wide brimmed straw hat and sporting a long grey beard. Was eagerly waiting my return.
'I was worried that you would not come back to us.'
'I would never have done that I love you and our girls to deeply. I cannot wait to get home I have all the riches and wealth in you, the girls and my extended family.'
'What about your 'best seller'?'
'Sam can deal with that.'
He put out his hand and held my hand; he was a man of few words and kept his emotions for the privacy of our home. The touch of his hand meant everything to me. I had laid the past to rest; 'I love you', I whispered. He squeezed my hand tightly; 'home boy, take us home.'
'Holmes County is where I belong,' I thought, 'the big city and life in the fast lane is not for me.'

'Mammy Val's Little Book of Allsorts'

Recipes

Note: I have already mentioned on the back cover that all the recipes I will print here must have been tried and tested by my grand-mother but, I myself, have not done so with the exception of just a few. The first recipe below is very special to us as a family; it was a favourite of mine whilst growing up and from the time when my husband and I got married in 1959 grand-mother would make this as our Christmas pudding as neither my husband nor myself liked the usual Christmas Pudding; it was also served with the traditional brandy sauce; yum, yum mu mouth is watering. The recipe she kept secret and it was only in her latter years did she give it to her great niece. If asked what were the ingredients she would always remark that they were a secret and that is why the pudding was referred to as a 'Puzzle Pudding'. She continued to make this pudding up to her 98th year and from that time and up to the present day I have been the one who made the pudding; not just for Christmas but on the request of my family.

So in memory of my grand-mother 'Gwenllian' I won't keep it a secret any longer – do try it I am sure you will enjoy it with white sauce or custard.

Gran's Puzzle Pudding

2 cups of breadcrumbs
1 cup of Atora Suet
1 cup of Self-raising flour
4 tablespoons of raspberry jam (use any jam but red jam usually makes a darker pudding – I found that 'jelly' jam did not blend in well so would not advise using it)
1 teaspoon of bi-carbonate of soda
2 tablespoons of soft brown sugar
Just for Christmas I added a teaspoon of mixed spice.
Small quantity of milk

Mix bicarb, jam and milk together and add to the other ingredients.

Place in a greased basin, cover with greaseproof paper and then foil remembering to pleat the paper and foil as the pudding will rise. Tie with string and make a string handle to enable the pudding to be lifted from saucepan.

Place in a saucepan of simmering water and cover with lid.

Steam for two and half to three hours. Making sure that

the water is kept at half way up the basin.
Serve with white sauce or custard.
The quantities can be doubled – if so cook for slightly longer.

Enjoy!!!

Next another family favourite – made by my grandmother with vegetables from the garden – '**Dig for Britain**'

Leek and Potato Soup

For four servings you will need:

1lb. of leeks
1lb. of potatoes
1oz. of butter
1 pint of stock or water
Seasoning
Half a pint of milk
3-4 tablespoons cream
To garnish a few leek slices or parsley; paprika

1. Clean leeks very thoroughly and slice; peel and slice the potatoes.

2. Fry vegetables in the heated butter over a low heat for about 10 minutes with the lid on the pan, shaking occasionally to prevent vegetables sticking.
3. Add the stock; bring to the boil, season to taste.
4. Simmer gently for approximately 30 minutes.
5. Keep back a few slices of leek for garnish.
6. Blend or sieve soup and return to pan with milk; re-heat
7. Add cream.

To serve; Pour into a tureen or individual soup bowls; garnish with leek slices and paprika pepper.

To vary: garnish with chopped chives or parsley.

Serve cold: using half a pint of extra milk or white wine to give a creamy consistency.

Glamorganshire Sausages

150 grams of fresh breadcrumbs
1 small leek; washed and very finely chopped
75 grams of Caerphilly cheese – grated
1 tablespoon of chopped parsley
Salt and freshly ground black pepper
Pinch of dried mustard
3 eggs – 1 separated
Milk for binding.
Plain flour
Extra breadcrumbs for coating
Oil or bacon fat for frying

Mix together the breadcrumbs, leek, cheese, parsley,

seasoning and mustard. Beat together 2 of the eggs and 1 yolk and use this to bind the mixture; adding a little milk if the mixture is too dry to hold together. Divide into twelve portions, form into sausage shape and roll in flour. Beat the remaining egg white until frothy, brush this over the sausages and coat in extra breadcrumbs. Chill for 20 minutes. Fry gently until crisp and golden brown on all sides. Serve immediately with chutney or relish.

A Variation of Bread and Butter Pudding

There are numerous variations to the following recipe –
sweet or savoury;
Savoury: cheese and ham; cheese and tomato; cheese, ham and tomato. Haven't tried tuna and sweetcorn. The choice is yours I am sure you will have plenty of ideas.
Sweet: Your favourite jam; fresh fruit; vine fruits etc..
Perhaps one could use brioche I haven't tried this.

Take 6 slices of medium white bread
One and a half ounces of butter
3 thick slices of cooked ham
3 tomatoes thinly sliced
Salt and pepper – a small quantity of dried mustard could

be added if desired.

1 pint of milk

Oven setting: 350 degrees F or Gas Mark 4

Remove crusts from bread; spread bread with butter. Place slices of ham and tomato on 3 slices of bread; retaining a few slices of tomato for garnishing; then top with remaining slices buttered side up.

Beat together eggs (using a wooden spoon will beat in more air and make a lighter custard), salt, pepper and then blend in milk; strain over bread and garnish with tomato. One could use grated cheese and make a cheese sauce.

Cook in a moderate oven for 35-45 minutes until 'custard' is set.

Gran's Christmas Trifle

4 trifle sponges; 8 macaroons; 8 ratafia biscuits; One and a half ounces almonds; 1 banana (fruit of your choice) half a pint of custard, clotted or double cream, fruit juice or sherry, strawberry jam; angelica, cherries.

Make the custard and cool it; spread the sponge cakes with the jam and arrange them with the crumbled macaroons and ratafias in a pretty dish. Pour over a little fruit juice or sherry to soak them well; add the sliced banana (a drop of lemon juice will prevent banana going brown) and the almonds that have been blanched and chopped; pour over the custard lightly pile cream on top of custard and garnish with cherries, angelica and almonds.

Another trifle:

Black Forest Trifle

You will need: Chocolate flavoured Swiss roll; a tin of black cherries; blackcurrant jelly; chocolate blancmange; double or whipping cream.

Slice Swiss roll and cover bottom of a pretty serving dish; soak with juice from cherries and then place cherries on top; make up a chocolate blancmange and leave to cool – covering with greaseproof paper to prevent skin forming – when cool pour onto fruit and leave to set; whip cream and decorate as desired.

Gran's Christmas Cake

She has written on the recipe 'very rich'.

One and a half pounds of currents;
One pound sultanas or raisins or half and half.
Half pound of mixed peel;
2 ozs of sweet almonds;
6 eggs;
12 ozs of p
2 tablespoons of milk;

Four tablespoons of brandy;
Half a pound of butter;
Half a pound of brown sugar.

Beat butter and sugar to a cream; add eggs one by one beating well; sieve flour and add gradually; add fruit (thoroughly cleaned) – **note: no prepared fruit in the days when gran baked this cake.**

Add spice, brandy and flavouring (almond or vanilla essence can be added if desired). Put in a well-greased and lined tin and bake in a moderate oven for four hours until a skewer comes out clean when tested – **note gran would cook this in the oven on the side of the fire.**

Almond Paste for Cake:

Half a pound of ground almonds;
10 ozs. of fine white sugar (icing sugar?)
2 eggs;
juice or 1 orange and 1 lemon and any other flavouring desired.

Pound the almonds and
add eggs, well beaten and any flavouring beat well and then knead with hands; roll out to fit top of cake.

I wonder how many of you, if feeling poorly, would sample some of gran's recipes?

Special Vitamin Broth

Half a cupful of celery stalks
Half a cupful of celery tops
1 cupful of carrots scrubbed but not peeled.
1 cupful of green cabbage
1 tablespoon of chopped parsley
1 tablespoon of chopped watercress
4 cups of water

Grate and shred all vegetables as finely as possible put in saucepan with water and simmer for 30 minutes; add a dash of celery salt and onion salt if desired. This quantity is enough for two generous servings – taking half at mid-day; cooling the rest. At 6.00p.m. reheat slowly and add half a cupful of tomato juice.

This special broth will always give you a boost; taken as a mid-day meal once a week to keep in trim.

Hot Weather Medicine

Two ounces of caster sugar
Two ounces tartaric acid
Two ounces of fine glauber salts (sodium sulphate)
Two ounces of cream of tartar
Mix all well together and put in a glass jar.
Dose – 1 teaspoon in a tumbler of water before breakfast
– an excellent 'cooling' medicine.

I wonder is it due to the fact that I was raised by my Victorian grandmother and her bachelor brother that I can still recall remedies used by them.

Dr. Williams' pink pills for pale people – claimed to cure Neuralgia; nervous headache; palpitations of the heart; pale and sallow complexions and all form of weakness in both male and female.

As my uncle was Edwin Williams he would jest that he was the doctor who invented this miracle cure.

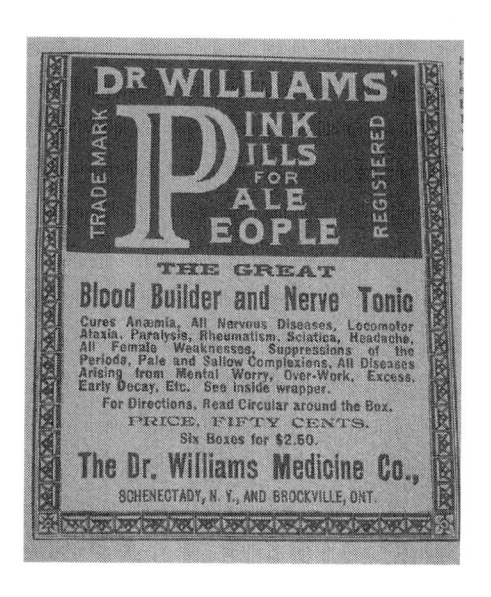

'Mammy Val's Little Book of Allsorts'

> **Nervous People.**
>
> Nervous people not only suffer themselves but cause more or less misery to everyone around them. They are fretful, easily worried and therefore a worry to others.
>
> When everything annoys you; when your pulse beats excessively; when you are startled at the least unexpected sound, your nerves are in a bad state and should be promptly attended to.
>
> Nervousness is a question of nutrition. Food for the nerves is what you need to put you right, and the best nerve food in the world is Dr. Williams' Pink Pills for Pale People.
>
> They give strength and tone to every nerve in the body, and make despondent, easily irritated people feel that life has renewed its charms. Here is proof:
>
> Miss Gem Waterus, the sixteen-year-old daughter of Mr. I. C. Waterus, of N. Chapen St., Bradford, Pa., was stricken with a nervous disorder which threatened to end her life. Resident physicians advised the trouble was from impoverished blood, but failed to give relief. Mr. Waterus heard of Dr. Williams' Pink Pills for Pale People, worked hard and saved enough to buy a box and try them. After using six boxes her appetite returned, the pain in her head ceased and she was stronger than ever before. 'My daughter's life was saved by Dr. Williams' Pink Pills for Pale People,' said Mrs. Waterus. 'Who confirms the above from time to time when approached taking them, but your skin is strong and healthy. I cannot recommend these pills too highly.' — *Bradford (Pa.) Era.*
>
> Most druggists are reliable. Some are not. A dealer who tells you that he has something just as good as Dr. Williams' Pink Pills for Pale People is unreliable. Insist on having the genuine. At all druggists, or sent postpaid by the Dr. Williams Medicine Co., Schenectady, N.Y. on receipt of price, fifty cents per box; six boxes, $2.50.

Weekly Banner, 28 April 1899, p. 7, cols. 5-7.
©Athens-Clarke County Heritage Room, 2010

Another was Beecham Pills – the advertisement said 'Worth a guinea a box.'

Val Baker Addicott

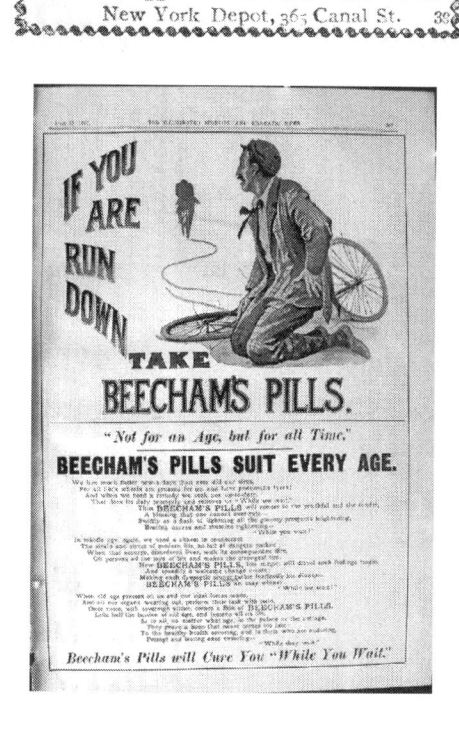

One that is still available today but with the drugs no longer in the medicine is Dr. Collis Browns Chlorodyne – claimed to have been used in the boar war and a cure for everything: it contained opium and chloroform (no wonder the patient slept). The dose was a maximum of 15 drops. Believe it or not I was given this in its original form when I suffered from migraine at a very young age (it worked well). It was said that it was a cure for coughs and colds; asthma, bronchitis, cholera, dysentery, diarrhea, toothache etc..

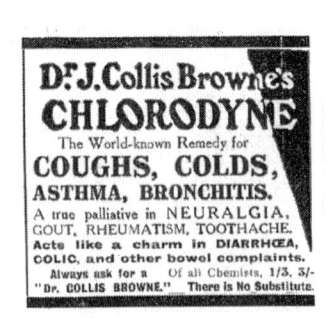

Dr J. Collis Browne's
CHLORODYNE
The World-known Remedy for
COUGHS, COLDS,
ASTHMA, BRONCHITIS.
A true palliative in NEURALGIA, GOUT, RHEUMATISM, TOOTHACHE.
Acts like a charm in DIARRHŒA, COLIC, and other bowel complaints.
Always ask for a Of all Chemists, 1/3, 3/-
"Dr. COLLIS BROWNE." There is No Substitute.

I remember my grandmother brewing Senna ponds as a laxative for my uncle; and dosing me up with good old Syrup of Figs

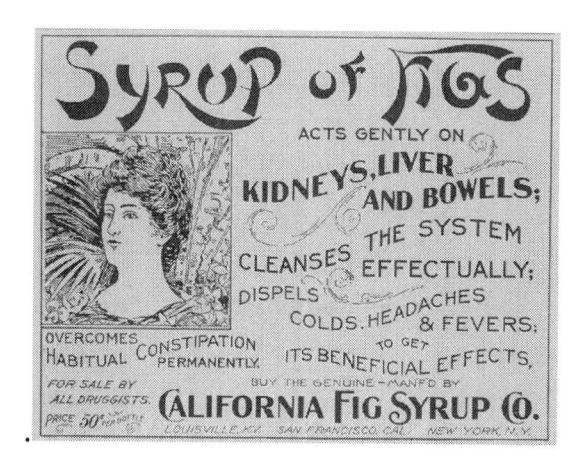

I recall a time when I had had a tooth extracted and it bled profusely and as grandmother thought I was looking pale she bought be ox blood tablets that I had to chew – can't recall if they did any good but they were horrible. Think she did this because I wouldn't take Parishes Food. Being above average height for those days and quite thin the old biddies in the village would say 'she's out grown her strength.'

Coming in after being out playing in the snow – feet soaking wet and freezing cold I was given a bowl of warm water in which gran would put a few crystals of permanganate of potash; the crystals would emit a pinky lilac colour in the water and I would soak my feet; was it the soothing warm water that warmed my feet and prevented a chill or was there any good in gran's remedy? I suppose it was a mild form of antiseptic. Sometimes gran used some dry mustard powder; if too much was added one was inclined to have yellow feet.

There was no mention, in those days of my childhood, of allergies; any rashes if not diagnosed as contagious were treated with bi-carb. A paste was made for insect bites and on one hot summer's day when I was plastered in a rash a handful was put in my bath – the old tin bath and a bucket on the fire to warm the water. The rash soon disappeared – another miracle cure!!! I wonder how much good, if any, were in these old remedies?

Not exactly a remedy but Lux soap flakes put in the tin bath and the water then poured over made a lovely lather – better than all today's bath salts etc.. The mention of 'salts' brings to mind the use of smelling salts when one felt faint or sal volatile.

A few more 'miracle cures' that I haven't

mentioned:-

> **How does she Keep so SLIM & Lovely**
>
> She simply can't help attracting attention with her clear skin, radiant health and slender figure. She keeps in perfect health by taking Bile Beans each night at bedtime. These fine vegetable pills keep the blood pure, tone up the system and prevent unwanted fat forming. So follow her lead and look and feel your very best
>
> **By Taking Nightly**
>
> **BILE BEANS**

'Mammy Val's Little Book of Allsorts'

Take Care..
Colds-Susceptible!

An eminent physician states that of the 60,000 preventable deaths yearly in the U.S., many are due to neglect in treating the common cold. It is vitally important, therefore, that colds be kept under control.

In thousands of clinical tests, under medical supervision, Vicks Plan for better Control of Colds has greatly reduced the *number* and *duration* of colds—has cut their *dangers* and *expense*. The Plan provides proper care and medication, at the proper time and place, for different types and stages of colds. (Full details in each Vicks package.)

**When Colds THREATEN
... VICKS NOSE DROPS**

Heed that first warning sneeze, sniffle or nasal irritation. Quick!... Apply the new aid in *preventing* colds, Vicks Nose & Throat Drops. Gently, they stimulate the functions which Nature has provided—in the nose—to throw off threatening infection.

**If a Cold STRIKES
... VICKS VAPORUB**

If a cold has developed, massage throat and chest at bedtime with VapoRub. Acting through the skin, like a poultice, VapoRub "draws out" tightness and soreness. All night long, too, its medicated vapors carry soothing relief *direct* to irritated air-passages.

VICKS PLAN FOR BETTER CONTROL OF COLDS

Val Baker Addicott

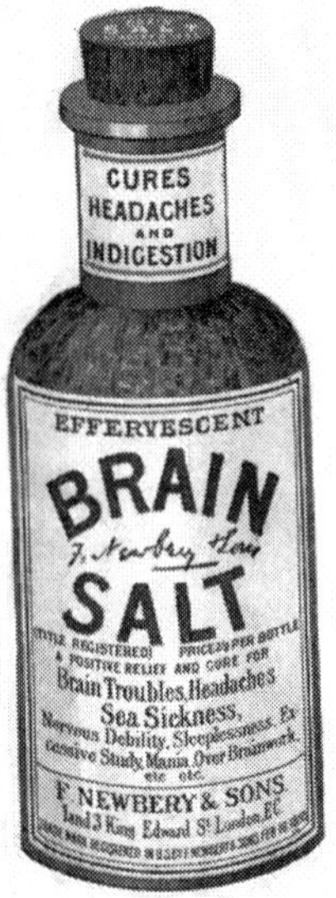
CURES
HEADACHES
AND
INDIGESTION
EFFERVESCENT
BRAIN
SALT
A POSITIVE RELIEF AND CURE FOR
Brain Troubles, Headaches
Sea Sickness,
Nervous Debility, Sleeplessness, Excessive Study, Mania, Over Brainwork,
etc etc.
F. NEWBERY & SONS

Quick facts for the busy Doctor about

GENUINE PHILLIPS' MILK OF MAGNESIA TABLETS

EACH TABLET CONTAINS ONE TEASPOONFUL OF GENUINE PHILLIPS' MILK OF MAGNESIA IN CONCENTRATED FORM.
30 TABLETS   PRICE 25¢

1. Phillips' Milk of Magnesia Tablets are actually made from genuine, concentrated Phillips' Milk of Magnesia.
2. They are not to be confused with dry-form combinations of magnesium oxide, magnesium carbonate and calcium carbonate now on the market.
3. Each tablet contains 4.8 grains of precipitated magnesium hydroxide, or an amount equal to one teaspoonful of Phillips' Milk of Magnesia. This concentration is 13 times as great as in U.S.P. liquid Milk of Magnesia.
4. They therefore have the marked effectiveness in neutralizing acids that Phillips' Milk of Magnesia has.
5. They offer a new convenience for the small, frequent doses which thorough alkalization calls for. Can be carried easily in pocket, hand-bag or traveling-bag and taken wherever and whenever necessary.
6. They are as pleasant to take as candy mints which, indeed, they taste like. They melt quickly on the tongue and leave no after-taste.
7. Here, at last, is a form of this remarkable antacid which you can prescribe and be sure your patients will readily accept.

IN SLENDER, LIGHT BOXES OF 30.....
Handy to carry in vest pocket or hand-bag.

IN BOTTLES OF 60.....
A supply for the family medicine cabinet and traveling-bag.

Gran claimed to be a 'teetotaler'- as a young woman she was an avid follower of the 'Band of Hope' – a Christian and Temperance Society – so it amazes me on looking through her old recipe books that there are so many recipes for wine making. I remember her making elderberry wine. Again I will mention I am just going to print the recipes as found in her note books; they have not been tested by me.

Rhubarb Wine

5 pounds of rhubarb; 1 gallon of cold water; 4 pounds of loaf sugar; 2 lemons. Half an ounce of isinglass.
Cut rhubarb into small pieces and bruise it. Put into a pan with the water. Let it stand for five days; stirring three or four times a day. Then strain the juice, add sugar, grated lemon rind, to the juice add the isinglass. Let the liquid remain for four or five days until fermentation subsides. Skim and strain and put in a cask. Keep airtight; bottle in six weeks.

Hock Wine

2 oranges; 2 lemons; 6 potatoes (uncooked) sliced; 1 lb. of raisins; 4 lbs. Demerara sugar; 1 gallon of warm water; yeast the size of a walnut; pour the warm water over above ingredients; pull open the raisins when lukewarm; add yeast spread on toast let it work for two weeks; take off the froth and strain. Bottle and gradually tighten corks after it has ceased working.

Elderberry Port

3 pints of ripe berries; half an ounce of hops; 3 pounds of sugar; 1 pound of raisins; small amount of yeast; 1 gallon of water. Put hops, berries into a thin muslin bag; boil for half an hour; take out bag squeezing out all liquor; then boil sugar and liquor for 10 to 15 minutes. When nearly cold 'work' with a little yeast spread on toast. Cover and stand for three days; well skim put into a jar with the raisins;

Vessels should be of wood or earthenware or glass and must be clean as any germs present will multiply rapidly in wine and will turn it sour. Cork loosely until finished working; bottle and store.

Elderberry Wine

The elderberries must be ripe and picked on a dry day.

Put a gallon of elderberries in a gallon of cold water and bring to the boil – boil for 30 minutes.

Strain off the liquor, measure it and to each gallon add 3 pounds of Demerara sugar, half an ounce ginger and quarter ounce cloves.

Boil for another half an hour, pour off the liquor and when it is lukewarm add compressed yeast on a piece of toast, allowing half an ounce of yeast to every 3 gallons.

Fermentation should begin in about twenty-four hours. Let the liquor stand for three days and then cask it. Let it stand for four months before bottling when it is ready to drink because elderberry wine does not need such long keeping as most other wines. Nice drunk hot. This recipe gran used in 1934.

I remember how some bottles would 'explode' in the cupboard where gran had stored them; 'corked down too early', she would say.

Another Elderberry Wine recipe

1 gallon ripe elderberries; 4 pounds granulated sugar; 1 ounce of bruised ginger; 1 ounce of cloves.

Place the berries in 1 gallon of cold water and allow to soak for 9 days. The berries should ten be skimmed off and the other ingredients added with the exception of the sugar. Bring to the boil and then add the sugar. Leave to stand for 12 hours before bottling and two days before corking.

Blackberry Wine

Place the fruit into a cask or pan and pour boiling water over to cover allowing 1 gallon of water to every 4 quarts of berries (about 4 pounds) when cool press the fruit with your hands then let it stand covered until the pulp forms a crust on top (about 3 days) then add 3 pounds of sugar to each gallon; put a piece of toast spread with yeast and leave it work for about a week. When it has ceased working the whites of two eggs may be added to clarify it or a little isinglass dissolved then added to the wine. Strain and bottle.

Blackberry Cordial

To one quart of blackberry juice add 1 pound of white sugar; 1 teaspoon of cloves, allspice; cinnamon and nutmeg; boil all together for 15 minutes add one wineglass of brandy or rum. Bottle while hot; cork tightly and seal.

Gran's Hints on Wine Making

Always use good materials and measure accurately – too much or too little may spoil the wine; use half an ounce of yeast to the gallon and add it when the liquor is lukewarm and let it work until fermentation begins to cease. Temperature in storage cupboard is important this should have an even warmth from 55 to 60 degrees F. Cloudy home-made wine can be cleared by adding isinglass half an ounce to the gallon. Dissolve it in a little of the liquor; this is done by standing the basin in hot water then distribute amongst the wine in the bottles or pan; should leave undisturbed for a month. A handful of raisins and a little brandy will improve the flavour of wine; add barley sugar for additional sweetening.

Vessels should be of wood, earthenware or glass and must be clean as any germs present will multiply rapidly in wine and will turn it sour.

Bottles should not be filled or they may burst in warm weather; store them on their sides. Home-made wine will sometimes turn sour owing to being kept at too high a temperature or it may suffer from a deficiency of alcohol or an excess of albuminous matter; this can usually be remedied by the addition of isinglass or white of an egg.

Gran's notes 1934.

'Mammy Val's Little Book of Allsorts'

Merlin

I closed my eyes and the vision I saw brought to me great happiness; I was sitting at the feet of my beautiful mother, who was nonchantly twisting my ebony ringlets through her fingers; I wore a beautiful blue broiderie anglaise dress and a had a large satin bow of ribbon in my hair It was one of those golden, halcyon days of a summer now long gone but one that would always remain in my memory. Mother was so beautiful; father always referred to her as his Dresden China Doll; her skin was like fine porcelain and to protect herself from the summer sun she sat on the garden bench under a parasol that gave her protection from the sun's strong rays. The view was panoramic; as from our large home and grounds we had a beautiful view of the Cornish coast. Father came striding along the lawn; he appeared, to me as a child, to be so tall and handsome in a rugged kind of way. He bent over and kissed mother and placed in her hand a single red rose; 'shouldn't you be resting, my sweet?' He questioned.

'Do not worry so my darling I will rest later when Vi has her music lesson.'

I guessed that father was concerned about mother as I had been told that I would be having a baby brother or sister when the summer was over and I was to return to school. There were so many things that I didn't understand; I had heard mother and father talking to the doctor and he had been telling mother to 'take things easy' as she had 'lost' two babies; how could one lose a baby?

The scene changed; like a mist on Bodmin Moor, it was a dark, ominous cloud that blotted out the sun. Father had sold our grand home and we now lived in a squalled place near Penzance; I no longer wore pretty dresses and now my beautiful hair was matted and tangled. The change had taken place after mother had died giving birth to my baby brother; they had both been buried in the church-yard near Tintagel. Father was broken hearted and he took to consoling himself in drinking liquor. He got into bad company and began to gamble and within a year we had to sell the house. It had been a long arduous trek to Penzance but father said he knew some-one who would give him work. There was worse to follow; one afternoon, when I was about thirteen, father brought home a gentleman; I assumed he was a gentleman as he was dressed in fine clothes like father once wore.

'Vi always remember that mother and I loved you so much;' his words upset me as he hadn't mentioned mother since the day of her burial and had hardly spoken any kind words to me from that day; he continued, 'you are going to live with Mr. Murphy he has kindly offered to employ you as scullery made.' I could see that father was trying to hold back tears.
'I don't want to go and live with Mr. Murphy I want to stay with you.'
'Get moving child I haven't got all day;' he pushed me towards the door.
'Treat her well Shaun.'
'I paid you well for the brat by cancelling your debts to me; she is mine now and I can treat her as I wish; get out of my way,' again he pushed me; harder this time that I nearly fell. 'Don't get yourself into more trouble;' was his last retort to my father; 'I won't be there to help next time.'

We travelled for what seemed miles in his fine carriage; I had started to cry but refrained from doing so as he had kicked my leg with his riding boots. When we did finally stop it was outside a fine mansion and I heard that we were not far from Truro. From that very moment I was treated badly, how I longed to return to my father. I was more or less dragged into the kitchen by the coachman.
'The Master said to feed the brat and then shove her in

the room above the stable until he decides what he is going to do with her.'

That cloud stayed with me and seldom did it allow the sun to shine through. I worked as a scullery maid and did all the dirty jobs that no-one else wanted to do. I had a meagre ration of food and was beaten by the house-keeper if she saw me idling. When I first started my cycle I was frightened that I was dying yet it brought relief to me that it would be the end of my life of terror but a maid told me it was natural and it was a sign that I was becoming a woman and advised me to stay away from dirty old men or I would end up in the work-house. I understood very little of her explanation. At that time each month the house-keeper was even crueler as she would lock me away in my stable room until the period had stopped. All I had was straw on the floor and a few old sacks that gave me very little warmth on cold winter nights and a bowl of icy cold water to wash and a bucket.

Almost three years I suffered this torture; for that is what it was. It was a hot day at the end of summer when I was sitting in the yard cleaning all the dirty boots when I overheard an argument.
'If I want to 'take' you in the afternoon I bloody well will.'
'The baby Shaun you might harm the baby; my time is near.'

I heard my Mistress scream out; I was naïve as the day I was born; no-one had told me what went on between man and woman. What had the master done to make his wife scream so loudly?

'You fat bitch,' he yelled, 'if you can't satisfy me I'll get young Vi in my bed she is ripe for the picking; there will be fun and games then after I have broken her in.'

His words rung in my ears and I recalled what the maid had said about staying away from 'dirty old men.'

I made up my mind there and then that I was going to 'run away'; but where could I go? Then an idea flashed across my mind; I had heard the stable boys talking about a circus that was in town and they were going to go on the final Saturday before it upped-sticks and moved onto the next town. I had remembered going to the circus with mother and father and they had said that the circus people were 'travelling folk' and I remembered father jesting that as a boy he always wanted to 'run away' and join the circus. Today was Sunday and in the distance I could see the trail of caravans moving along the highway. They would surely pass by about a mile from where I was now standing. I ran to the stable rolled up in a sack a piece of stale bread that I saw lying on the stable floor and a handful of oats that was the horses feed and from which I had ate for quite some-time. The only possession I had was a photo in a silver frame of mother, father and myself taken at Christmas-time a year before mother died; this I had kept well hidden. I glanced around and it appeared that everyone was busy; the family visiting friends after Sunday Mass; Sunday Mass that in itself was a joke to me as I wondered what the priest would have said if he knew how they were treating me. I hadn't been inside a Church since mother's funeral; we always went as a family every Sunday and often lunched with the vicar and his wife and family; those were such happy days; would I ever be happy again?

I started off at quite a brisk pace but the further I walked I began to slow down; my feet hurt and I could see that they had begun to bleed as the thin leather on the sole of my shoes had worn away and there was a big hole in the bottom. Obviously, the slower I walked the further into the distance the circus seemed to disappear. It was getting quite late; 'surely', I thought they would stop for the night and then I would be able to catch them up. 'It must be early evening', I thought as the sun was sinking fast in the west. The evening came upon me so quickly as one minute there was a cloudless sky and the next the sky became grey and overcast. I had no idea of where I was and I could no longer see the circus; I had been following what my father would have called a 'sheep track' quite a distance from the road and now I began to wonder had it veered further away; I saw a few sheep grazing and in the distance some ponies how I wished that I could catch one and not have to walk any longer. I was so tired and although I saw sheep I could not see any sign of a farmhouse or shepherd's hut. The terrain that had once been rough beneath my feet now began to feel marshy and along the edges where there had been heather and grass there now grew reeds. If only I could find a place to shelter until morning then a new day would bring better views of how the land lay. I kept stumbling over my own feet but managed to keep going but then I tripped over something on the path and felt myself rolling down a bank; I tried to pull myself back up but each time I appeared to slip further back. I had had enough, if no-one came along the path I would die and be in heaven with my beloved mother; that would most certainly be better than the life I had in servitude. Thinking of my mother made me cry and I recollected her words 'that life was precious'. If I lay still perhaps I could sleep and with a new day find a way to get out of my predicament. A mist had fallen and seemed to shroud me as it swirled about. If there were reeds and such wet earth surely I must be nearing the shore; could the circus have been heading for St. Austell? I tried again to pull myself up from the hollow by crawling forward on my hands and knees I didn't slip back this time but exhausted collapsed.

I felt myself being lifted up; had the angels ascended and were carrying me to heaven but on opening my eyes I

screamed. It was the devil himself who was carrying me off to Hades; had I been that wicked that the angels weren't sent for me. In the glow of a lantern I saw a being in a dark cape and a large black hat; very little of a face was visible as it appeared to be on fire.
'Well, Ned what have we found here?'
My fear calmed a little when I saw the horse and the fire on the man's face; for that is what he was; was just his 'red' beard and whiskers. His voice was also soothing and comforted me as he sounded like father.
'Did you get left behind by the circus lass?'
'No' I whispered; 'I was running away from my master and was trying to catch up with them but I was too slow and lost sight of them.'
'You poor little one; you have wandered miles from the main route to St. Austell where the circus was heading. It was a good thing that you did stumble because the path you were taking would have led you into the marsh and the lake and there are also many treacherous areas that would have sucked you down.' He put me down in the back of the trap and taking off his cape put it over me. 'I'll take you to my humble abode and in the morning we will journey on to my sister who lives in Newquay. What shall I call you little one?'
'My name is Vi; father said that mother was such a romantic that she named me Viviane but I have always been called 'Vi'.
The man roared with laughter; why was my name so

funny?

'I am known as 'Merlin' I believe my little Lady of the Lake we were fated to meet.'

I knew well the Arthurian legends as mother had often related them to me; was my rescuer really Merlin the Magician?

'I am known locally as Captain Red Davies as I travel the vast oceans and seldom spend time in my home.

He called to the horse; 'Home boy' and I felt the movement of the trap rock me into a dream like stupor. I pulled his cloak over my shivering shoulders and nestling my face into the course fabric I could smell his masculine odour. It made me feel safe; it seemed to cast a spell over me and gave me the feeling that this man would not harm me. How had he found me? He had appeared, as if by magic, from nowhere. If he had been travelling behind me surely I would have noticed him but there again perhaps not as the mist had come down quickly and visibility had been poor. What if he hadn't found me would I have endeavoured to continue on and be sucked down in a peat bog? I must have fallen asleep as when I opened my eyes I was being lifted from the trap and Merlin was calling out to someone called Zac to take the horse to the stable. The moon was high in the sky so I guessed we must have travelled some distance. As he strode across the yard realization dawned on me that every bone in my body was aching and the worse hurt were my feet.

'Jesse', he called get the kettle on 'I found a wee lass lost on the moor.'

I wondered was Jesse his wife; I didn't want him to have a wife so hoped that Zac was her husband. Merlin was my knight in shining armour and as I nestled close to him my heart began to beat faster.

He put me down on what appeared to be a bed in a cupboard and from there I could see a roaring fire in the hearth and on the table an oil lamp burned brightly; two children appeared from another room; 'Mother who has Merlin brought home?'

'A little lost soul; now back to bed with you.'

'Her feet need bathing Jesse; they will bleed all over your bedspread.'

'First things first; come my dear drink this broth you need some good warm food; why, you are nothing but skin and bone; worry not about the bedspread it can be washed.'

The hot liquid burnt my throat but it was the best food I had had in ages.

'Take her to the chair by the fire Merlin while I fetch a bowl.'

He gently lifted me up and carried me to the chair; how I longed to stay nestled in his strong arms.

'The poor lass has no soles left on her shoes no wonder

her feet are bleeding.' The woman knelt down and gently bathed my feet; at first they hurt even more but soon the pain eased. She then dried them carefully and put on some soothing balm. Merlin stood close by watching over me; until she said 'off with you Merlin go and help Zac in the stable; I need to get the lass out of her clothes and into a night shift.'

I nestled down under the patchwork quilt; I so loved the comfort of the feather bed and soon I felt a warm glow come over me and also a feeling of contentment. How long I slept I do not know but I awoke in a bath of perspiration and a horrible pain in my head that made me cry out. 'What bothers thee?' Jesse asked.

'I have a pain in my head and I am so hot.' I cried.

'My, my you are on fire;' she tried to get me to drink some cold water but I felt to weak and lay back down exhausted now all I wanted to do was sleep. 'Merlin' I called but it must have been just a whisper as Jesse did not respond.

I could smell his body odour and I felt the roughness of his coat against my face; I was safe again.

'She can't stay here Jesse she has a fever and until we know what is wrong you must think of yourself and your unborn baby and the children. Zac can drive me back home and then go on to Newquay and pick up my sister as she will know what ails the child; I am supposed to be setting sail the day after.'

'Mammy Val's Little Book of Allsorts'

I could hear his words but didn't have the energy to open my eyes; he called me a child didn't he realize I was a young woman; I didn't want him to leave I wanted him to stay with me for-ever I had never felt so safe as when I was in his arms. Was it the fever that burned through my body or the pain in my head that made me elucidate? I had called out to him and again he had come and saved me; he really must be Merlin the Magician or how else would he have known that I wanted him?

How long had I slept? I awoke to see the sun shining in on me and I was lying in a large bed just like the one mother and father used to sleep in; then I noticed the wallpaper it appeared like shining gold as the sun cast its light upon it; the gold was the colour of the trellis and climbing the trellis were large red roses. For a moment I gazed in amazement at my surroundings if this was Merlin's home he must be very rich and then my eyes filled with tears as I thought of him sharing the bed on which I lay with his wife; for surely he must have a wife.
'Good morning Vi you have had us so worried; I must go and tell Merlin that you are awake.'
Was that plump, pretty little woman Merlin's wife? I had noticed though that she had the same red hair as Merlin; then I remembered that I had heard him saying he would send Zac for his sister.
'Good morning my Lady of the Lake it is so good to see you looking so much better.'

'How long have I been sick?'

'Almost a week; the doctor has been out to see you every day as you have been very poorly; he said that between the neglect, at the hands of your employer, and your perilous journey on foot all those miles it isn't much wonder that you ended up with pneumonia.'

'I thought I heard you say you were sailing on the morrow?'

'I couldn't leave until I knew you were well. As soon as the doctor says that you are fit to travel we will go back to my sister Elaine's home and then once you are settled in I must make plans to leave.'

I wanted to cry out that I didn't want him to leave; had he cast a spell over me I felt hypnotized by his very being; I longed for him to pick me up in his arms; I wanted to nestle close to him and feel his strong arms around me. He was magic; he had read my mind. He leaned over the bed and picked me up in his arms; he was so strong it was if I was a baby in his arms.

'Elaine said it would give you more pleasure if you lay on the sofa under the window and then you could see across the garden.' He gently put me down and wrapped a rug around my legs.

'I love the garden it is so pretty. Will you live here when you come back from your voyage?'

'I will be gone for many months this time so I have sold the house as it is too much for Jesse to look after with a new baby due any day.'

'Where will Jesse and Zac go?'

'They have been with me for many a year so I have given them their cottage and a few acres of land; they are sad to see me leave but obviously pleased to now own their own place and not have to answer to the new owner.'

'Why do you have to leave?'

'I have a contract to take our Cornish tin to lands far across the seven seas and sometimes I also take passengers as many are looking to better their lives in other countries.. I must leave now as I have work to oversee upon the ship so I will see you at supper and I do hope the doctor will leave me a good report.' He leaned over and kissed me gently on the brow; 'it is good to see the roses coming back into your beautiful face my little one.'

Within days my life changed completely; he took me to his sister's guest house; I felt completely at ease with her; the only thing that showed that they were siblings was her shock of flaming red hair; other than that she was small in stature where Merlin was quite tall and her waist line seemed to match her height. Elaine had already prepared an attic room for me as she kept the other rooms for her visiting guests. The delightful attic room had lace curtains draped on the two small windows and the most comfortable of single beds that had upon it a beautiful crocheted throw there was a small dressing table with a

delft ware jug and basin and soap dish and one cane chair with a heavier crocheted patchwork rug and on the wooden floor boards there was a hand-made rag mat of pretty blue and cream pieces of cloth. I placed on a little bed-side table the photo of myself with my parents; how glad that through all the trials of the last weeks it had survived. What most impressed me was the view from the small attic windows as I could gaze out upon the azure waters and watch the fishing boats and larger vessels anchoring in the harbour. How I longed to get down to the shore line and sit in the warm summer sun.
Merlin had told me that when I was fully recovered I would be expected to assist Elaine with the running of the guest house. This I thought would be such a delight to help this lovely lady; I guessed that she might be a little older than her brother and put her age at about thirty.

I cried myself to sleep the night after Merlin set sail on the afternoon tide. He had given me a big hug and kissed me lightly on the cheek. 'I will return' he had said but hadn't said 'when'. His sister later told me that sometimes Merlin was gone for two or more years. How could I possibly live with his sister and not daily think of him. It had been a new experience for me feeling a tingle through my very being when he had held me in his arms; if only for a fleeting moment. Was this longing I felt for him telling me that I had fallen in love with this wonderful man?

I must admit I was happy living with Elaine; she treated me as a younger sibling and although I made beds and washed and cleaned no chore was too difficult or too strenuous and also she would send me out shopping on an afternoon and when the weather was good she would tell me to take a walk and enjoy the fresh air that would put roses back in my pallid cheeks.

Once I was fully recovered I enjoyed walking along the cliff tops even on a stormy day. The bracing sea air brought Merlin closer to me as I thought of him standing at the helm of his ship and guiding his vessel over the monstrous waves. I prayed every night for his safe return. As I stood and watched the high waves and white sea-horses what really caught my imagination was the blow hole in the cliffs at Trevelgue Head; the old folk told tales that Bronze Age man had lived in the area and my imagination would run wild that they might have stood where I was standing and watched the stormy seas.

I would sit on the harbour wall and watch the fishing boats returning with their catch of herrings and pilchards and the big ships returning with their cargo of rocks that were turned into quick-lime in the lime kilns in the harbour.

Every-where was a hive of activity; walking down South Quay Hill I would watch the large schooners being built. Coal, limestone, timber and grain were brought in by ships and as I sat and watched I would look far out to sea and hoped and longed for the day when I would spy Merlin's ship on the horizon.

Weeks turned into months and months into years. Elaine had received long over-due letters; he had asked Elaine to give me his best wishes and he hoped that I was well and happy.
Each Sunday come rain or shine Elaine and I would walk to the Chapel of Ease in Bank Street; dedicated to St. Michael. It was very 'new' as Elaine would say and all the work of Rev. Nicholas Chudleigh who had laid the foundation stone in 1858 and the new church had opened the very same year in the September. Dressed in my Sunday best, bought with money left by Merlin for my up-keep, I felt really pretty something that I hadn't felt since those days in the big house with mamma and papa. I had many admiring glances and I know a few young farmers and lads that worked in the harbour had asked Elaine for permission to 'court me'. Looking back I think that Elaine must have wondered why as some were very eligible young men but I knew where my feeling lay; but were these feeling just for the man who saved my life or did they go far deeper? I have already told you I had no knowledge of the 'love' of a man and a woman but one thing I did know that with each ship that came into the harbour and none were Merlin's I felt that my heart was

breaking in two.

The second Christmas came and went and still no word of Merlin's return. The little guest house only had one guest so there was very little work for me to do. I found in the New Year that this guest and Elaine had become very close; so each afternoon I would wrap up warm against the elements and take myself off across the cliff tops. Passing along the way the little row of white houses and the coastguard station that had been built in 1825. I would often spend time chatting to the 'old sea-salt' in the Watch House; he would tell me tales of smugglers who left their haul in the Tea Caverns under the cliffs at Gazzle and how a hundred horses would be waiting on Crantock Beach even on the Sabbath to pick up the contraband. When I asked him why he sat there looking out to sea he said it was his job to still watch for smugglers; ship wrecks and any invading forces. He also watched for the sighting of shoals of pilchards and then the little boats would go out and let down their nets; a big business in Newquay. Storms brought out the lifeboat that was launched off Towan Beach and what a task that was for man and beast as it was brought down on a carriage pulled by horses and hauled off by men in order to save lives. Every ship-wreck brought tears to my eyes and a pain in my heart; where was Merlin? When would he return? The silver frame now held a photo of the man that I held so close to my heart; I had found it in the drawer in my attic room and as Elaine never ventured up the steep stairs to the attic my secret was safe. Dare I tell you that each night after I had knelt and said my prayers I placed a kiss upon his face; 'May God protect you and bring you home to me.' It never entered my head; well, if it did I soon cast such thoughts aside, that he might have a wife and family in some distant land and would never return.

March came in like a lion but the blustery winds did not deter my walks along the headline. Easter that year came early and after Church on Easter Sunday Elaine took my arm as we walked back home. 'Be happy for me Vi; Thomas has asked me to marry him.' She took her glove off her left hand and there sparking on her third finger was a diamond ring. I didn't care who was watching as I put my arms around her and gave her a kiss; 'I guessed you were more than 'just good friends' as you so often told me; I wish you all the happiness in the world.'
'I had a letter from Merlin; he was leaving the New World at the end of April and hopefully he will be home by June when we plan to marry. He also sends his best wishes to you and asked were you being courted. I will still 'run' my little guest house; the little attic room is yours for as long as you wish as you are such a great help to me.'

From the middle of May I spent hours sitting on the headland watching the schooners and large ships enter the harbour. Elaine had had no further letters from Merlin but her hopes were high and the bans were called in the Church and plans were made for the wedding to take place on the longest day; the summer solstice. There was a magical feeling in the air that made me think more and more about Merlin and how he had seemed to have appeared from no-where when he saved me from death's door. If I closed my eyes and called his name would he hear me? Would when I opened my eyes see his ship on the horizon. It was such a beautiful evening; the sky was cloudless and the sun, like a ball of fire, was setting in the west. I lay on my back in the heather and gazed up to heaven; the stars were just beginning to peep. 'I really must be getting home' I thought, 'Elaine will be worrying about me.' Still I lingered; one star shone brighter than all the others; words that I had read on a postcard came to mind. 'Star light, star bright; the first star I see tonight; I wish I may, I wish I might; Have the wish I wish tonight. I wish,' I started to say aloud but hesitated; what if someone heard me; sitting up I looked around but there was no-one in sight; again I said 'I wish, I wish for Merlin to sail into the harbour; please star shining bright grant my wish tonight. Merlin, Merlin come home to me;' I called his name and hoped that it would be carried on the breeze. Dusk was falling quickly so I got to my feet and hurried back along the cliff path taken him away from Newquay.

'I've hired a horse and trap as I thought you might like a trip to Tintagel; I believe you said you once lived nearby.'

'I'd love to,' I said, 'but I had better go and change my dress.'

'There is no need; you look so pretty wear it for me; it was just bought for the day.'

'Surely it will take too long it is over twenty miles.'

'I've arranged rooms for us in a local inn. I thought it would give you a chance to visit your mother's grave.'

One minute I felt elated the next at the thought of my mother I felt near to tears.

The scenery was pleasant as we travelled along the country roads and lanes; catching glimpses of the azure blue sea as the lanes twisted and turned. Our conversation was jovial but really it was about something or nothing; I learned nothing of his life as a seafarer. He told me he had been to the New World; and that it was a vast nation; its people of many races and creeds.

As we entered the gates to a large house memories came flooding back; surely this was the house where I was born; I saw the rolling lawns and the path that led down to a small bay; I closed my eyes and remembered as a small child playing on the sandy beach, I held back my tears but Merlin noticed and taking my hand he said; 'I'm sorry I made you cry little one perhaps it was rather thoughtless of me to bring you here; it is no longer the home you remember it has had many alterations as it is now a hotel.'

The front entrance was just as I remembered, as was the vast hall except for a small area that now housed a desk where it appeared that visitors registered.

'Your rooms are ready Mr. Davies said an elderly lady who was sitting behind the desk.

'Thank you Maud.'

'No luggage Sir,' said a young lad who was dressed in the uniform of a bell-boy.

'Not this time Joe, just a fleeting visit.'

Everyone seemed to know him and he appeared to call them all by their Christian names.

'Have you stayed here before?' I asked.

He laughed; 'I own it.'

As we entered what looked like a cage to me I felt it suddenly moving and when it stopped we were on another floor. Everything appeared to be newly decorated and the carpet below my feet felt so luxurious. Another bell-boy opened a door that led into a room and from the view at the window I recognized it as my parent's room but everything had changed; the wallpaper, the light fittings and the small anti-room that had been mother's dressing room was now a bathroom; what luxury.

'Rest a while and I will knock on your door when it is time for dinner which will be about seven o'clock.'

'Dinner', I thought, 'surely he meant supper.'
I slipped off my dress and my pretty slippers and ventured into the bathroom; what a surprise awaited me there were soft white towels and sweet scented soaps and pretty glass jars of bath salts. I had seen such pictures of these items in papers that had been left at the guest house but never thought I would ever wash in such fragrant soaps. Then I began to wonder if I was to stay the night in this room I had not brought a nightdress. Turning back the bedspread before lying upon the bed I found a pretty nightdress on the pillow; it reminded me of the pretty nightdresses mother had hand sewn for me when I was a child.
I was too excited to rest as so many thoughts were going through my mind. The main one being Merlin and why had he brought me here? If his thoughts were of seducing me he would not have arranged separate rooms. I must admit I was rather disappointed as from what I had read in books my body was sending out so many signals and I was ready for love. Then I thought of Elaine and recalled her saying that she had kept herself 'pure' until her wedding night. Had she been trying to tell me to remain a virgin until my wedding night? Why was I thinking such thoughts Merlin had only ever kissed me on the cheek in a brotherly fashion and never had he mentioned any words to show he had feelings other than brotherly ones for me?

I noticed from the ornate clock on the mantle-shelf that it was gone six o'clock surely I hadn't fallen asleep. I quickly got up and tidied the bed; why had I bothered tis was now a hotel; I was afraid to venture into the big bath so just quickly washed my face and hands and put some cream from a pretty pot on my face; well the label did say 'face cream'; I noticed a brush and comb on a side table so undoing the bow that tied back my hair I quickly combed it through and re-tied the ribbon. Lastly, I slipped on my brides-maid dress and sprayed on some lavender scented perfume from a bottle standing on the same little table. The clock now said six forty five and I was ready and I must admit feeling rather excited of dining in what was now most luxurious surroundings.

I heard the awaited knock on the door to my room and eagerly rushed to open it.

'Viviane, my beautiful Lady of the Lake, may I escort you to dinner?' As he hooked his arm in mine a shiver ran down my spine. 'I think I had better warn you I have one more surprise for you.'

What could it possibly be? I felt quite excited, had he brought me here to propose to me? He led me towards a table by the window and as we approached a man, who had his back to us, rose from his chair and as he turned I gasped and as I felt Merlin's arms around me I fainted.

The smell of the smelling salts under my nose revived me and then I heard Merlin's words; 'Vi, my darling Viviane I am so sorry I didn't think I just thought it would be a lovely surprise for you as so often you have said that you wondered what had happened to your father. I met him a few weeks ago when visiting Bath to arrange a booking for Elaine's honeymoon and your father was managing the hotel. I asked him would he like to run my 'new' hotel and when I told him it was his old home he was delighted to accept. I have put him in full charge of the running of the hotel as I set sail for the Americas the day after tomorrow.

There was a mixture of sadness and joy in Merlin's words. Sadness that again he was leaving with no words to me that he would ever love me; yet had I heard him calling me 'darling'? There was also great joy in being reunited with my father; there was no denying that in the years we had been apart he had aged but to me at this moment in time he looked more like my beloved father than the last image that had remained with me of a drunken, broken man I had been taken from almost six years earlier.

Dinner was served by smartly dressed waiters and with the exception of a glass of wine I had had at Elaine's wedding breakfast I had never tasted wine before so it was new to my palate and I think made me feel rather merry; we had so much catching up to do and then Merlin dropped another surprise.

'Elaine and Thomas have decided to sell the guest house and I thought it would be nice for you to come and live here with your father; there will be no rush but when you are ready just let your father know.'

I slept very little that night; the moon shone brightly in through my window and the stars sparkled like myriads of diamonds. My wish had come true he had returned home but not to stay he was sailing far away again and out of my life. We only had one day left and he had promised to take me to Tintagel the legendary birthplace of King Arthur and where Merlin performed his magic on Uther Pendragon. How I wish that I, like Viviane of Arthurian legend, was able to perform 'magic' on Merlin and bewitch him into never leaving me.
I was sad at leaving my father but promised that within the month I would arrange to move to the hotel. Tears filled my eyes as I hugged and kissed him 'goodbye'.
I had tried to remove the creases from my dress but on putting it on I no longer felt like the princess I had felt the previous evening. I hadn't bothered to tie back my hair and as we drove along the coastal path my hair blew wild in the breeze.
'You are so beautiful,' he said as he brought the horse to a stand-still on the grass just a few yards from the ruins of Tintagel Castle. I was about to step down when his arms were around me as he lifted me down; for a moment he held me close; I lifted my face and looked into his dark brown eyes how I longed for him to kiss me but the moment was lost but what had I seen in his eyes? It

appeared to be a deep sadness.

His mood changed as he stood on the rocky out-crop and after looking out to sea he turned and recited these words:

'I must go down to the seas again; to the lonely sea and the sky; and all I ask is a tall ship and a star to steer her by, and the wheel's kick and the wind's song and the white sails shaking; and a grey mist on the sea's face and a grey dawn breaking. I must go down to the sea again for the call of the running tide; is a wild call a clear call that may not be denied; and all I ask is a windy day and the white clouds flying, the flung spray and the blown spume and the sea-gulls crying. I must go down to the sea again to the vagrant gypsy life, to the gull's way and the whales way, where the wind like a whetted knife, and all I ask is a merry yarn from a laughing fellow rover, and a quiet sleep and a sweet dream when the long trick is over.'

I applauded him but there were tears in my eyes as I felt it was his way of telling me that he had to go to sea as it was his way of life; the only way he knew.

'Did you write those words?' I asked

'No', he replied but there was a sadness upon his voice; a poet by the name of John Mansfield. 'My sweet Lady of the Lake do not shed tears over me. I want to love you but it will be no life for you to be left for months and perhaps even years as I sail the seven seas. Perhaps, I should have said that I do love you and I want to make love to you and hold you in my arms from sunset to sunrise but how can I make love to you and perhaps leave you with my seed within your womb and you good name lost to you forever.'

Together we walked back to where the horse and trap stood; no words were spoken between us; I for one didn't know what to say. I wanted to cry out 'I love you, I want you to make love to me and I don't care about my good name.'

We sat with our backs against the trap and unpacked the lunch that had been prepared for us but my appetite for food had left me and had been replaced with an appetite or perhaps I should say a yearning to feel his body next to mine. 'I have to sail on the morning tide my ship is already laden with a cargo.'

I wanted to hide my longing so I jokingly said, 'I suppose you have a woman in every port that satisfies your needs. You don't care how I feel about you and how those feelings have grown since our first meeting. I can still smell that same body odour I smelt when you put your coat over me in the trap and when you picked me up in your arms. Don't you care that I too have feelings and that I love you and long for you. Can't you take me to sea with you?'

As if my words had hit him like a thunder bolt his arms were around me and his lips were upon mine; no longer was it a brotherly kiss it was what I had been waiting for.

'No my Lady of the Lake I do not have a woman in every port I have had you on my mind and close to my heart from that very first day I found a poor little lass drowning in the mire.' We lay together in the long grass and his kisses grew more passionate and then he pulled away from me for just a moment as he undid the buttons on the front of my dress; how can I describe the feelings of an innocent virgin as he fondled my breasts that tingled with his every caress. He lifted the skirt of my dress and as I felt his fingers touch those secret places known only to me I moaned with pleasure; between his kisses and his caresses I knew that my body yearned for the final act and realized that even in my ignorance of love making I knew that he too was ready to enter me as his manhood was hard against me. 'I love you,' he said as he started to undo the belt of his trousers, 'I want you my darling Viviane.'

It was not to be for as he raised my dress and lay upon me the horse moved towards us and would have trampled over us if we hadn't quickly moved. The moment was lost as was his erection. We laughed it off but then he turned to me and said; 'perhaps it was for the good.'

We travelled back to Newquay in silence; I wanted to put out my hand and touch him I wanted him to want me; to stop the trap and make love in the back where once I had lay with his coat over me. I knew he was aware of my feelings. As the evening brought a sudden chill I shivered and as if reading my previous thoughts he stopped the trap but not to take me into the back to make love but to take off his coat and put it over my shoulders.

He reined in the horse outside the guest house and getting down he opened the door; I made no attempt to get down as I wanted just one more time to feel his arms around me surely then the longing would return and he would carry me into the house and to bed where we would make passionate love until the morning. Before returning he lit a candle in the hall. 'Are you staying there all night?' he teased. He came around to my side and lifted me down and for a fleeting moment he held me close but there the closeness ended. He did not carry me into the house or even to the doorway. 'Do not come down to the harbour to see me off I shall be gone before you awake. My little Lady of the Lake find someone to love you as you should be loved.'

'I will never stop loving you and no-one else will never take your place.'

'Never is a long time.' He said and before leaving he kissed me longingly on the lips. 'I do love you and always will. Goodbye sweet Viviane.'

I was tired and heart-broken and longed to sleep but as dawn broke I stood at the window and watched him sail away into the distant horizon. 'Merlin, Merlin,' I cried, 'come back to me.'

It would be two days before Elaine and Thomas would be returning. Would things have been better for me if I could have 'cried' on Elaine's shoulder? There was nothing for me to do in the home; everything was neat and tidy. I decided I would do some shopping on the day of their return so feeling so depressed after watching Merlin's boat disappear into the far horizon I got back into bed and burying my face in the pillow I cried and cried and felt as though my heart was broken in two; well as far as I as concerned it was. I felt it was pointless to get up so there I stayed all day and as dusk fell I stood by the window and gazed out to sea and again I called his name 'Merlin come back to me; I want you and I need you; I love you Merlin.' The thought of him and the picture of him on my bedside table started me crying; it wasn't worth me living without him; why, oh! Why had he saved my life only to end up breaking my heart?

If I was to go and live with my father I may as well go as soon as Elaine and Thomas returned. They wouldn't want me 'playing gooseberry'. Unable to sleep I took down a wicker case from on top of the wardrobe; I had examined it when I first had come to live with Elaine and knew it was empty I decided to pack my clothes and the few possession I had accumulated. Because of the generosity of Merlin in supporting me I now had quite an array of clothes. Then I thought, perhaps I should leave them behind as I had arrived with nothing so should I leave with nothing? On the top of the case I placed Merlin's picture in the silver frame. I had an urge to remove it as it really wasn't mine and just leave the picture of my mother and father and myself taken in those happy childhood days. My thoughts were in turmoil; why had Merlin bought my old home: why had he installed my father as maître d'hôtel? He must have cared a great deal about me to have done that; yet not enough to leave the sea and marry me.

I was hungry but I couldn't bother to eat breakfast so picking up the shopping basket and taking some money from the old tea caddy I made an early start to the shops. I would prepare them a lovely meal and then send a message to father to come and pick me up. I really hadn't considered everything as my only thought was getting away from Newquay and by doing so I would not see the ocean going vessel in the harbour and therefore, close my mind to Merlin. If I had thought it through I would have realized that living in my old home, although, it had changed greatly it was still full of memories and from every window in the front of the great house one could gaze out upon the sea and in doing so Merlin would remain close.

By early afternoon I had prepared everything and leaving a note to welcome them home I decided to take a walk across the cliff tops to clear my mind of all my silly thoughts. It had been a beautiful morning but within an hour after leaving home the weather changed. I recalled what the 'old salts' would say; 'sea mist coming down so quickly means that a storm was brewing.' Why did everything remind me of Merlin? Even down to the sea mist on that treacherous day when I lost my way. I really must turn back or surely I would get lost or even the worse could happen if I came too close to the cliff top. There were unusual noises echoing on the air; a rustle as of an animal walking over the heather; a loose rock rolling down the hilly surround; was it the sound of a horse's breath that echoed in my ears. I began to feel frightened as one didn't live in such a community without hearing tales of ghosts and the 'ancients' who lived here centuries before. Were the dead that were buried on top of the cliffs rising to haunt me? I began to feel icy cold and as I shivered goose-bumps crept down my arms and down my spine; then the hairs on the back of my neck began to stand on end and when a hand grasped me on the shoulder as if to push me to the ground I screamed and called; 'Merlin help me'.

'Not this time you whoring bitch he is far out at sea.'

The voice sounded familiar but before I could utter another word his hand was across my mouth and he pushed me to the ground. 'I've been following you for weeks and now I can get my reward you escaped me once before but this time there is no-one to save you. I

would have liked to have been the one to have 'broken you in' but Davies had the pleasure of doing that.'
It was then I realized that my attacker was the horrid Shaun Murphy.
The sea mist had become quite dense but I could see the man who now had his foot upon my belly. I tried to move but as I did so he pressed his foot down hard upon me. I could see in the dim light he was undoing the buttons on his trousers; he moved his foot but before I had chance to move he was on top of me. He pressed his mouth hard against my lips and because I made no response he bit deep into my lips.
As his hands tried to reach beneath my clothes I tensed my leg muscles and held my knees together.
'Open your legs you bitch I'm ready for you.' He shouted obscenities at me; 'I'll take you one way or another; how would you like me to cut your throat. He pulled open my blouse and grabbed my breast. I had to stop him, he was hurting me but as I moved he forced my legs apart.
'Merlin, Merlin;' I screamed. I felt him hard against me but then as if a gale force wind had suddenly blown up he was torn from me; I was free. I rolled over and tried to get up but every bone in my body was hurting. Then I heard a gun being fired and a horrendous scream and then there was silence. Who had fired the shot? Had anyone been killed? I tried again to get to my feet and then I felt myself being lifted up.
'My darling, my sweet little Lady of the Lake I was a

fool to leave you.'

'Merlin,' was all I could say before I fainted.

I awoke in my bed with Elaine fussing over me, bathing my lips and putting a herbal balm upon my painful breast.

'Merlin' I said he is a magician he heard my calls and came to my rescue.'

'I like that thought,' said Elaine 'but it didn't quite happen that way. He had trouble with the engine it wasn't getting up enough steam and decided to return to harbour. He came looking for you and saw the note you had left for me and decided to go and meet you. All I can say is thank God that he did.'

'I heard a gun-shot what happened to Murphy?'

'Merlin fired and hit Murphy but had no intention of killing him but Murphy turned on Merlin and a fight broke out and during that fight Murphy lost his footing and went over the cliff-top. When the tide turns his body will soon be found and the crime of murder will be put on Merlin as he was seen walking along the cliff path. His engine has been repaired and he is ready to leave.'

'No! No!' I cried, 'he cannot leave without me.'

'He has no intention of leaving without you. He has paid a lad to take your box down to the harbour and now that you are awake and I have done all I can you too must leave because by noon the police will be looking for you as well as Merlin as you are aware you spoke to people as you left the town and headed up the path to the headland. God go with you Viviane and protect you and Merlin from all harm one day I am sure we will meet again.' She hugged me and kissed me and with Thomas by my side I made my way to the harbour. I was still trembling after my ordeal but now I began to shiver as thoughts raced through my head; what would happen to us if we were caught? Surely Merlin, if found guilty, would be hung or even if there was no case against him the possibility was high that he would be sent to Botany Bay even if the death was an accident.

I was helped aboard a small boat and as the boat was rowed from the shoreline I looked back and could see just a flicker of a candle in my attic room. I remembered Elaine's words; 'I will keep a candle burning for you to light your way back home.' As we came alongside the ship I looked up and saw Merlin holding a lantern and at the same time I noticed the rope ladder. Was I expected to climb that? I was guided by a young sailor and slowly I made my way to the top; exhausted I collapsed into Merlin's arms. 'Hush, hush my darling don't cry I promise everything will be all right.' His cabin below deck was far better than ever I had anticipated. 'Make yourself 'at home'', he said as he put me down on his bunk bed.
'Where will you sleep?' I questioned.
'I can string up a hammock on the bridge.'

'Don't leave me I am so frightened.'
'There is no need to be afraid you are safe now. I have to leave you for just a short while until we are safely out into the Atlantic. You are still trembling my love; I will send old Walter with something to warm you; I promise I will be back as soon as possible.' He kissed me on the cheek and lightly touching my swollen lips he said; 'no-one will ever hurt you again my sweet Viviane.'

I lay upon the bunk fully dressed; old Walter brought me a steaming bowl of what appeared to be some form of soup and the young sailor, a mere lad of no more years than thirteen, brought my wicker case. I was too tired and now my body and sore legs seemed to hurt even more. I must have fallen asleep but something had disturbed me; I opened my eyes and found Merlin lying by my side and he was gently smoothing my hair.
'Merlin,' I said, 'my body hurts so much.'
'Why don't you undress and put on your night shift the soft material will help to soothe your tender body.'
'I haven't the energy and the pain is so bad.'
He rose from my side and gently helping me to sit up he removed my coat and then my blouse and skirt. 'Elaine has given me some balm to soothe your sore body are you able to apply it or shall I?'
My arms were covered in bruises and every movement made me want to cry but how could I let a man apply

balm to my breasts and stomach and to the bruises on my inner thighs?

I watched as he poured some solution into a bowl and then he came and sat by my side and so very gently bathed my sore and still bleeding lips. 'How I wish I could kiss them better.'

His gentle touch was to me, at that time, like a butterfly kiss. Putting the bowl down he did not ask again but undid the ribbons on my bodice and very gently slipped it off my shoulders; I felt my colour rise as I realized I was almost naked; a silly thought came into my head I wondered how he would have managed to undo all the hooks if I had been wearing stays. As he rubbed the balm in my breasts it was as if by magic he had taken away the pain; after the horrific experience I had had only hours before how could I now have a longing in my groins for Merlin to make love to me. My thoughts, or was it Merlin's touch made my nipples harden; I wanted him so much I lay motionless as he pushed down my bloomers to rub the soothing cream on the bruises on my stomach where that beast had trod upon me.

'Damn the bastard may he rot in hell.' Merlin said as he moved away to put down the almost empty jar.

The only bruises left that hadn't had the soothing balm were the ones on my thighs. I recalled that Elaine had said they were the most painful.

I panicked when I saw him undoing the straps of my case as I knew that on the top he would see his photograph.

'I know very little about lady's attire so can I assume that this is your night shift; I think I can see here some of my sister's fine needlework.'

Was he just making conversation to cover his embarrassment? I too was beginning to feel embarrassed as it had been hours since I had relieved myself; how was I to ask him where could I go? I must have blushed crimson as I asked; 'where can I go to pass water?'

'There are facilities behind the screen.' He helped me to get to my feet and before he had a chance to slip my nightdress over my head my bloomers dropped round my ankles. I sat back down to remove them but as I went to lift my leg I cried out in pain.

The oaths that he uttered on seeing the bruises I cannot repeat. He lifted my legs back onto the bed and forgotten was my need to use the facilities behind the screen as every touch of his hand took away the pain but it brought on a new pain, a throbbing and a longing more intense than when we almost made love at Tintagel.

'I love you,' I whispered.

'I love you too my beautiful maiden. I want you now but how can I make love to you I do not wish to cause you more anguish. I will lie with you until you fall asleep and dream my Lady of the Lake my sweet Viviane of the time when I will make you mine.'

He helped me to my feet as nature called and when I very slowly and very painfully returned to the bunk I found he

had removed his clothes; I gazed in wonderment at his fine physique; and could not turn my eyes away from his erect manhood. Why does one have stupid thoughts at such momentous moments? I could not but wonder how it could possibly penetrate me? For a moment he held me close then turning back the rug he lay me down and then lying next to me he began to caress my body. I wanted to put my hand out and touch him but although his caresses, at first, excited me soon I began to feel drowsy; the warmth of his body next to mine was a comfort.
'Sleep my little one, sleep.'
Sleep I did; not just until daybreak but well into the afternoon, I awoke to see the sun streaming in through the porthole and I then I saw Merlin sitting by a desk on which were rolled up papers and many nautical instruments.
'Merlin,' I called, 'I thought I had dreamt it all but it is real I am at sea with you.'

I cannot recall how many days passed before I felt strong enough to get dressed; I lay upon the bunk in my nightdress conscious of the fact that beneath it I was naked. Old Walter brought me food; a form of gruel for my breakfast and it seemed that all he could cook was soup or stew. Merlin worked in the cabin he told me that he was plotting the ship's course and all the many instruments helped him and he also kept a daily log of all activities on board the ship. I don't know if he was afraid of the consequences but he spent no further nights with me.

He walked with me on deck; showed me the big boiler room and the stack of coal that fed the big gaping and ever hungry mouth of the boiler. He stood behind me and held my hands as he let me turn the ship's wheel. My bruises were now turning purple and as my lips healed they began to crack with the salt air old Walter gave me some cooking lard to grease my lips. How glad I was that there were no gale force winds and no rough seas. I chatted with the crew and heard many tales of their adventures on the Seven Seas. How they had all nearly lost their lives rounding the Cape; how pirates had fired at them in the South Seas. The 'cargo' they hated carrying were the prisoners bound for Botany Bay. I shivered at the thought that this very ship could have been taking my beloved in chains to Botany Bay.

I had not counted the days as time had been lost to me at the beginning of the voyage but surely it had been more than three weeks since we had left Newquay. One morning I was awakened with a kiss from Merlin.
'Put on your pretty blue dress today and pretty yourself up as today is going to be special.'
Before I had time to ask 'why' he had left. I gazed out of the port-hole and could see a flock of gulls diving into the sea and flying high overhead. I wondered were we

reaching land and was that the reason why Merlin wanted me to dress in my best.

Another surprise awaited me when Merlin returned to the cabin in his best naval uniform. 'We are about to dock in Boston Harbour a good friend of mine will be waiting for us.'

As I stepped up on deck I hadn't been aware that a day could possibly be so hot. The ship had already docked and below on the quay stood a great number of people. So this was New England; I was awe struck not just by the people but by the number of ships in the dock. I had always assumed that the ship Merlin sailed was his but it was only when I saw him in his fine uniform that he told me he was a captain in Queen Victoria's navy. There was so little I knew about the man who I loved so deeply. I waited on deck with Merlin who stood by my side with his arm around my waist holding me close.

'Permission to come aboard.'

'Permission granted.'

I saw a man in naval uniform sporting a finer set of whiskers than Merlin and following him on board an elegant mature lady dressed in fine silks and wearing a huge hat and carrying a parasol to protect her fair complexion from the strong rays of the sun.

'Viviane may I introduce you to Admiral and Mrs. Edward Stevenson.'

I didn't know if I should take the Admiral's out-stretched hand or curtsy to his wife. I had never met such important people.

The admiral's wife must have noticed that I was ill at ease as taking my hand she said; 'Let us go below deck out of this heat.'

A young girl, whom I hadn't noticed, followed us. She seemed to be struggling to carry numerous boxes and on arriving back in Merlin's cabin all was revealed.

'What is happening today Mrs. Stevenson? I thought we were disembarking.'

'Please do call me Rose. I expect the men are having a tot of rum I think Merlin will need it I don't carry out his plans. He has left it to me to tell you that today is to be your wedding day.'

I just stared at her in utter disbelief; and all I could mutter was 'how?'

'I offered to buy you a bridal gown but Merlin insisted you had a dress that he wished for you to wear; he suggested that I bought a blue bonnet as blue as the lake by our home and pretty velvet slippers. My girl will dress your hair and perhaps add a little colour to your sallow cheeks. All Merlin has told us is that you have been through difficult times.'

'Surely he couldn't have sent all this in a message?'

'While you slept the ship docked and Merlin came ashore and spent the night with us.'

'How can we marry; the bans haven't been called and we are not American citizens.'

'You will marry on board this ship that is classed as English soil and my husband as a naval officer has the right to perform the ceremony. Come let us prepare you for your special day.'

My hair was brushed until it shone and tied back with a deep blue velvet bow. When it came time to slip on my own blue dress that I had worn to Elaine's wedding Rose muffled a cry of disbelief as my body was still covered with the fading bruises. The 'bonnet' was trimmed with lace and two ribbons hung loosely from the corners. I had tried to tie them but was told it was the fashion to let them just hang loosely. My slippers were also of deep blue velvet. I asked how had she known the right size and was told that Merlin had taken one of my slippers with him. Another large box revealed a posy of white roses tied together with the same deep blue velvet ribbon. All this had been bought this very morning.

'Come,' said Rose; 'your bridegroom awaits.'

As we walked across the deck the young girl held over me a parasol in the deepest of blue embossed with white roses.

Merlin was standing on the bridge and as I joined him his eyes lit up; and I heard his whisper; 'My Lady of the Lake.'

The only words I heard were Merlin saying 'I do' and my shy response as I promised to 'love, honour and obey him.' Then the final words; 'I now pronounce you husband and wife; you may kiss your bride.'

As we disembarked the crew showered us with rice and made an arch with their rifles for us to pass under. We dined in a very posh hotel and I assumed that it would be here that we would spend our wedding night but to my surprise as dusk began to fall over the harbour Merlin took me back to the ship. We were 'piped' aboard and cheers resounded across the deck. I learned that most of the crew had been given shore leave with only a skeleton crew left on board.
Merlin picked me up and carried me as he said 'over the threshold' into his cabin. Edward had arranged for champagne to be left on ice for us and Rose that the cabin was to be bedecked with flowers. I was in seventh heaven. I was now married to the most mysterious and magical man in the whole world and as far as I was concerned the most handsome.

He stood for a moment and held me at arms-length; 'do you know my darling that from the moment I first picked you up and carried you to my trap you cast a spell over me; I realized then that one day I would make you mine.'
'I too have kept a memory close to me; it was the smell of your body odour mixed with your pipe tobacco that remained with me and you still have that special odour. There are still questions I ask myself and have no answer and I suppose there is a rational reason but from that very first time you saved my life I have believed that you have

magical powers as when in times of trouble or great longing I have called your name you have as if by magic answered my call.'

'Call me now my darling if you have a great yearning for your lover; call me and I will come to you.'

'Sit by your desk and close your eyes and when I call come to me.'

'You play games with me; two can play at these games.'

I went behind the screen and quickly without any coyness removed all my clothes. Rose had given me some perfume and this I sprayed on my body. The thought of making love set my body on fire and my firm young breasts tingled with anticipation. Before I moved from behind the screen I called; 'Merlin, Merlin my lover where are you?' As I stepped into the room I saw him waiting for me and into his arms I ran both of us as naked as the day we were born. His lips were hungry for mine and picking me up he carried me to the bunk; his foreplay excited me and brought me to fever pitch time and time again; I wound my legs around him and pulling him close I was ready for him; I cried out like the gulls flying around the ship but my question had been answered everything was made for a purpose and nothing was impossible. We slept in each other's arms; we woke and drank champagne and made love until the sun shone in on us through the port-hole and then slept until noon.

'I have one more surprise for you my beautiful Lady of the Lake; today I will take you home.'

'How can we return to England?'
'Not to England my love but to the town of Plymouth in New England.'

It was the home I could never have imagined living in. Merlin took no more long voyages but had received instructions from England and took monthly tours around the coast of Canada. I was the perfect wife and Merlin the perfect lover. Our lovemaking intensified and there were no limits to how we found new ways to please each other. The following year we took a holiday away from the heat of the towns and journeyed up into the mountains. The small house we had rented beside a mountain lake was idyllic. We swam in the pure, clear cold water and made love in the long grass. We climbed to the top of the mountain and like two children we called out to Elaine our voices resounded from hill top to hill top. 'Do you think she has heard us?' I asked.

By the fall my wish that I had made one starry night by the moonlit lakeside had come true I was carrying Merlin's child.

Letters from home arrived frequently and Merlin was pleased to learn that the death of Shaun Murphy had been put down to accidental. That in a drunken stupor he had fallen from the cliff-top. No mention was made of a bullet wound. 'I don't understand that,' said Merlin 'I must have missed.'

Merlin, Viviane, and Elaine all part of the Arthurian legend so what else could we but call our son born the following May but Arthur. Merlin had instructions to return home so in the November we closed up our home and set sail for the Old Country. I already had a Christmas present for Merlin. The voyage was far from calm and the stormy weather and treacherous seas made me feel so sea sick. I spent most of the time in the cabin only going on deck when Merlin shouted Newquay ahead. It was early morning and from the deck I could see the light of a candle burning in the attic room. Elaine had wrote and told us that as the tourists were swarming into Newquay by train they had decided to keep the guest house.

We spent a wonderful Christmas but Merlin couldn't understand why, even on shore, I was still being sick every morning. I put him out of his misery on Christmas morning by telling him that by the summer Arthur would have a baby brother or sister. New Year was spent with father in the hotel; Elaine and Thomas joined us. Leaving Arthur with Elaine we wrapped up warm against the winter chill and took the trap to Tintagel.

'Shall we make love in the grass,' teased Merlin. If it had been springtime my answer would have been 'yes'.

We held hands as we gazed out to sea. 'One day said Merlin we will set sail again and return to the New World but for now our home is here in England's green and pleasant land.'

I know how much he loved the sea, it was in his blood, his new post was on the south coast and at the end of the month we were again picking up our roots and moving, quite ironically to Plymouth.

He kissed me passionately as we stood in the magical surroundings of Tintagel. We were lost in time he was Merlin the magician and I his Lady Viviane. We had cast a spell upon each other a spell that would bind us together for eternity.

NB:- All peoples' names in this story are fictitious

Poetry

'A Birthday'

Christina Rossetti

My heart is like a singing bird
Whose nest is in a water'd shoot;
My heart is like an apple-tree
Whose bows are bent with thick-set fruit

My heart is like a rainbow shell
That paddles in a halcyon sea;
My heart is gladder than all these,
Because my love is come to me.

Raise me a dais of silk and down;
Hang it with vair and purple dyes;
Carve it in doves and pomegranates,
And peacocks with a hundred eyes;

Work it in gold and silver grapes,
In leaves and silver fleur-de-lys;
Because the birthday of my life
Is come, my love is come to me.

Note: *Vair - Latin for variegated*

Someone Who Cares
Edgar Guest

This is what helps us our burdens to bear,
Deeply to love and greatly to care;
Friendships are many; the old and the new,
Laughter is a tonic and wise is the man who clings
To good humour as long as he can.
It isn't on money contentment depends;
It comes from our loved ones and faith of our friends.
Blest is the man who has love for sure,
With that to support him life's hurts he'll endure
And there is nothing so helpful in times of despair
As knowing there's someone who greatly will care.

The Vicar of Bray

In good King Charles' golden days,
When loyalty no harm meant,
A zealous High Churchman was I,
And so I got preferment;
To teach my flock I never miss'd,
Kings were my God appointed;
And damn'd are those who do resist,
Or touch the Lord's appointed.

And this is law, that I'll maintain,
Until my dying day, sir,
That whatsoever King shall reign
I'll be the Vicar of Bray, sir.

When Royal James obtained the crown,
And Pop'ry came in fashion,
The Penal Laws I hooted down,
And read the Declaration;
The Church of Rome I found would fit
Full well my Constitution;
And had become a Jesuit,
But for the Revolution.

And this is law, etc....

When William was our King declared,
To ease the Nation's Grievance,
With this new wind about I steered,
And swore to him Allegiance;
Old Principles I did revoke,
Set conscience at a distance;
Passive obedience was a Joke,
A Jest was non-resistance.

And this the law, etc....

When gracious Anne became our Queen,
The Church of England's glory
Another face of things was seen,
And I became a Tory;
Occasional Conformists base,
I damn'd their Moderation,
And thought the Church in danger was,
By such prevarication.

And this the law etc...

When George in pudding-time came o'er,
An Moderate Men looked big, sir,

'Mammy Val's Little Book of Allsorts'

I turned a Cat-in-Pan once more,
And so became a Whig, sir;
And this Preferment I procured,
From our new Faith's Defender,
And almost every day abjured
The Pope and the Pretender.

And this the law etc….

The illustrious house of Hanover
And Protestant succession,
To these I do allegiance swear,
While they keep possession;
For in my Faith and Loyalty
I never will falter,
And George my lawful King shall be,
Until the Times do alter.

And this the law, that I'll maintain,
Until my dying day, sir,
Hat whatsoever King shall reign,
I'll be the Vicar of Bray, sir.

Anon

Reputation
By William Shakespeare

Good name in man and woman dear my Lord,
Is the immediate jewel of their soul,
Who steals my purse, steals trash
'Tis something, nothing
T'was mine, 'tis his and has been slave to thousands,
But he who filtches from me my good name,
Robs me of that which not enriches him
But makes me poor indeed.

On First Looking into Chapman's Homer
By John Keats

Much have I travell'd in the realms of gold,
And many goodly states and kingdoms seen;
Round many western islands have I been
While bards in fealty to Apollo hold.
Oft of one wide expanse had I been told
That deep-brow'd Homer ruled at his demeane,
Yet did I never breathe its pure serene
'Till I heard Chapman speak out loud and bold;
Then felt I like some watcher of the skies
When a new planet swims into his ken;
Or like stout Cortez, when with eagle eyes
He stared at the Pacific and all his men
Look'd at each other with wild surmise___
Silent, upon a peak in Darien.

Our England is a Garden
By Rudyard Kipling

Our England is a garden, that is full of stately views,
Of borders, beds and shrubberies and lawns and avenues,
With statues on the terraces and peacocks strutting by;
But the Glory of the Garden lies in more than meets the eye.

Oh! Adam was a gardener and God who made him sees
That half a proper gardener's work is done upon his knees,
So when your work is finished you must wash your hands and pray,
For the Glory of the Garden that it may not pass away;
And the Glory of the Garden it shall never pass away.

The Rainbow
By William Wordsworth

My Heart leaps high when I behold a rainbow in the sky;
So was it when my life began; so is it now I am a man;
So be it when I shall grow old; or let me die
The child is father of the man
And I could wish my days to be
Bound each to each by natural pie

The Little White Road

The little white road climbs over the hill,
My feet they must follow, they cannot be still,
Must follow and follow, though far they may roam,
Oh! Little White Road will you ever come home?

The hills they are patient and steadfast and wise,
They look o'er the valley and up to the skies;
But you little road scrambles up them and over;
Oh! Little White Road you are ever a rover.

I fain you would go right down to the sea,
Where a ship with white sails will be waiting for me,
Go sailing and sailing to strange lands afar,
Where deserts and forests and lost cities are.

But when I grow weary of gypsying ways,
I'll sail home again to end all my days,

In a little white cottage beside a white hill,
But you Little Road will go wandering still.

I Wandered Lonely as a Cloud

I wandered lonely as a cloud
That floats on high o'er vale and hills,
When all at once I saw a crowd,
A host of golden daffodils!
Beside the lake, beneath the trees,
Fluttering and dancing in the breeze.

Continuous as the stars that shine
And twinkle in the Milky Way,
They stretched in never-ending line
Along the margin of the bay;
Ten thousand saw I at a glance,
Tossing their heads in sprightly dance.

'Mammy Val's Little Book of Allsorts'

The waves beside them danced, but they
Outdid the sparkling waves in glee;
A poet could not but be gay
In such a jocund company;
I gazed and gazed but little thought
What wealth the show to me had brought.

For oft when on my couch I lie
In vacant or in pensive mood,
They flash upon that inward eye
Which is the bliss of solitude
And then my heart with pleasure fills,
And dances with the daffodils.

By William Wordsworth

I Will Make You Brooches

I will make you brooches and toys for your delight,
   Of bird song at morning and star shine at night,
     I will make a palace fit for you and me,
   Of green days in forest and blue days at sea.

I will make my kitchen and you shall keep your room,
Where white flows the river and bright blows the broom.
And you shall wash your linen and keep your body white
   In rainfall at morning and dewfall at night.

And this shall be for music when no-one else is near,
   The fine song for singing, the rare song to hear!
   That only I remember, that only you admire,
Of the broad road that stretches and the roadside fire.

By Robert Louis Stevenson

Sayings and Words of Wisdom

If you need a friend, I'm sailing right behind
Like a bridge over troubled water,
I will ease your mind.

Paul Simon

Patience is a Virtue

The moon and the sun learned long ago that,
If each patiently waits its turn they will
Both have their chance to shine.

Susan Gale

To thine own self be true:-
And it follows as the night the day;
That canst not be false to any man.

William Shakespear

What a Wonderful World

I see trees of green…red roses too
I see 'em bloom…for me for you
And I think to myself…what a wonderful world.
I see skies of blue…clouds of white
Bright blessed days…dark sacred nights,
And I think to myself…what a wonderful world.
The colours of the rainbow…so pretty…in the sky
Are also in the faces…of people…going by.
I see friends shaking hands…saying 'how do you do'
They're really saying…I love you.

Louis Armstrong

I offer you peace,
I offer you love,
I offer you friendship,
I see your beauty,
I hear your need,
I feel your feelings,
My wisdom flows from the highest source
I salute that source in you
Let us work together for
UNITY and LOVE

Mahatma Gandhi

A mother's love reaches far beyond circumstances and feelings-----
It sees past flaws and imperfections-----
And celebrates God's gift of love,
Sent from heaven in the form of a child
Her children arise up and call her blessed.

Proverbs 31.28

This is the beginning of a new day;
You have been given this day to use as you will
You can waste it or use it for good.
What you do today is important because you are
exchanging a day of your life for it.
When tomorrow comes,
This day will be gone forever;
In its place is something that you have traded for it;
You want it to be gain not loss; good not evil; success not failure;
In order that you do not regret the price you paid for it
Let it be something good

'Our prime purpose in this life is to help others
If you can't help them at least don't hurt them.'
Dalai Lama

Give the ones you love wings to fly;
roots to come back
and reasons to stay.
Dalai Lama

'Mammy Val's Little Book of Allsorts'

Tried and Tested by my grandmother but not by me – some home-made chutneys and pickles.

Home-made Piccalilli.

Prepare 4 pints of vegetables – small onions; cauliflower; vegetable marrow; cucumber and some kidney beans.

Dissolve 3 heaped teacups of salt in 6 pints of cold water. Pour this over the vegetables and let stand for 24 hours and then strain off and heat the brine. When it is boiling add the vegetables and 6 tomatoes (skinned and sliced).

Boil gently for 5 minutes and then drain it well. In a separate vessel mix with a little vinegar 3 teaspoon of mustard powder 3 tablespoons of flour; 2 tablespoons of ground ginger and 2 teacups of moist brown sugar add this and a tablespoon of whole allspice and 5 pints of boiling vinegar.

Stir and boil gently until it thickens then add the vegetables, gradually. Continue to boil and stir for a few minutes after it boils. A little vinegar may be added if too thick. Bottle in the usual way.

Indian Chutney.

9 Large apples; 1 small Spanish onion; 1oz. of ground ginger; 2ozs. of salt; half an ounce of cayenne pepper; 2 ozs. of mustard seed; half a pound of moist brown sugar; 2ozs. raisins and 3 gills of vinegar.

Peel the apples and onions and cut into small squares. Put these into a saucepan and pour on the vinegar then add the remaining ingredients. Boil until vegetables are tender and then put into jars and cover loosely.

Mushroom Ketchup.

Take 1 peck of mushrooms freshly picked if possible. Break them into small pieces and cover with a layer of salt and leave for two days stirring occasionally. Then drain them through a sieve and to each quart add 3 blades of mace; half an ounce of black peppercorns; half an ounce of sliced ginger and 6 cloves. Boil the juice for a quarter of an hour quite slowly then add the spices and boil for 30 minutes. Strain and bottle when cold. Delicious with cold meats or fish.

Mustard Pickle.

1 vegetable marrow; 1 cucumber; 1 quart of small onions; 2 cauliflowers; 4 tablespoons of brown sugar; 1oz. of turmeric powder; 1oz. of mustard powder; half a pint of vinegar and a few chili seeds and cloves.

Wash and break up cauliflower; peel and cut marrow and sprinkle with salt and leave over-night then put all the vegetables through a mincer; place in a large pan with chili seeds, cloves, sugar and vinegar; bring to the boil and boil gently for 10 minutes. Mix turmeric powder and mustard with a little cold vinegar and stir into the pickle. Boil for another 10 minutes pour into jars and cover. This is ready when cold.

Tomato Chutney.

Three and a half pounds of green tomatoes; 1 teaspoon each of mustard seed, ground ginger and allspice; 1 medium sized onion; 10 cloves; 1 quart of best malt vinegar; 1 pound of brown sugar;

Method: Scald the tomatoes let them cool a little then

skin and cut them into small pieces. Put the tomatoes into a preserving pan with the spices and vinegar and when nearly boiling add the sugar and the whole onion boil gently for about two hours or until it looks clear and then remove the onion before it breaks into pieces. Turn the chutney into small pots and tie down like jam. If red tomatoes are used less vinegar is required.

Tomato Sauce.

3 pounds of tomatoes; 1 large apple; 1 small onion; 4 tablespoons of white sugar; 1 gill of vinegar; quarter of an ounce of ground ginger; quarter of an ounce of black pepper; 12 cloves. Boil in a pan for 20 minutes; strain and bottle.

Apple Chutney.

Boil 2 quarts of good brown vinegar with six pounds of good cooking apples (weighed after they have been peeled and cored) and 2 pounds of moist brown sugar until the apples are reduced to a jelly. The apples used must be juicy and good. Turn this into a pan and add 1 pound of sultans; 2 ounces of salt and 2 ounces of mustard seed and half an ounce of ground ginger and a quarter of an ounce of cayenne pepper and a few shallots cut small. The whole should be stirred daily for a week then put into wide mouthed bottles; covered with parchment and stored in a dry place.

Marrow Chutney.

6 pounds of marrow; One and a half pounds of onions; four and a half pints of vinegar; 3 pounds of cooking apples; one and a half pounds of loaf sugar; a few chili seeds and peppercorns; one and a half ounces of bruised ginger. Put spices in a muslin bag and boil all together for half an hour. Mix one ounce of turmeric; 3 tablespoons of cornflour with a little vinegar to a smooth paste boil quickly for 4 minutes after adding turmeric and cornflour. Bottle when cool and cork tightly.

Something Different.

Ox-heart Pudding.

Line a basin with suet crust; cut into small pieces one and a half pounds of ox-heart; slice in one onion and a rasher of ham. Dredge with flour, salt and pepper and add a little water. Tie up firmly and boil for 3 hours.

Pigs Feet Pie.

4 pigs feet; soak them well and stew until all the meat falls from the bones. Season well and place in a suitable pie-dish with gravy; cover with a nice flaky pastry and bake in a hot oven until pie is cooked. Delicious eaten cold.

Nourishing Soup or Jelly.

1 pound of veal; 1 pound of beef; 1 pound of mutton place all in 3 pints of water. Bring to boil and boil for 5 minutes then simmer for 6 hours add seasoning and turn into a mould it makes a nice jelly or it may be eaten as a nourishing soup.

Poor Man's Goose.

Half a pound of liver; 1 onion; 1 pound of potatoes; flour; half a teaspoon of sage; salt and pepper to taste. Slice liver and dip in flour and place the slices in a pie-dish; par-boil onions with sage and then pour over liver with sufficient liquid to come half way up pie-dish. Slice potatoes put over liver to form a crust and bake for one hour. This will be found most appetizing and equal to the taste of a goose.

White Soup.

1 Spanish onion peeled and sliced; 4 potatoes peeled and cut into pieces; 1 small cauliflower; 1 stick of celery washed and cut up. 1 pint of milk and 2 quarts of water; pepper and salt to taste.
Method: Put all the ingredients in a saucepan and boil until tender then rub through a sieve and put back into saucepan boil up and serve hot with fried snippets of bread.

Rabbit Brawn.

Take a young rabbit and boil until tender with some onions, carrots and a bunch of sweet herbs; cook so that the meat ca be stripped off the bones. When cold cut the meat and a quarter of a pound of cold boiled bacon into pieces. Wet a plain mould or basin and decorate with slices of hard-boiled egg and chopped parsley and then fill with the rabbit and bacon mixed; the meat must be well seasoned with pepper, salt and allspice and have a good sprinkling of chopped parsley. Strain some of the rabbit broth; season with salt and pepper and dissolve in it a little gelatin powder. Pour this while hot over the rabbit put a saucer or suitable utensil on top and a weight on top of that and leave until cold. Turn out and garnish.

'Mammy Val's Little Book of Allsorts'

Over the Garden Wall

My memory has only a small child's vision and overheard conversation of what the first five years of my life must have been like. Father held a very important government position in Whitehall and our home was a very large Victorian mansion in Park Lane. I can still picture my nanny whom I spent more time with than my parents. Mother was always entertaining; afternoon tea with her socialite friends; bridge parties and in the evening my parents always appeared to be going to one social event after another and when at home there were also endless cocktail parties. Dressed in her finery she would come to my nursery to kiss me 'goodnight'. I cannot tell if it is something I overheard or can I remember that if I put my arms up for a cuddle nanny would quickly pull me away saying; 'No child, no; your fingers are sticky and your mother is ready to go out.' One occasion I do recall; as mother bent over to kiss me I caught hold of her beads and the string of pearls broke and rolled across the floor; I remember it so well as nanny smacked me very hard across my legs and mother left the room crying. Life wasn't all bad as I so loved going into the park and feeding the swans and ducks on the lake; I saw other children playing; how they laughed and called out to each other as they hid behind the trees and sailed their boats upon the lake. Even at that young age I wondered why I wasn't allowed to join these happy children in their games. When I asked nanny I didn't understand her reply; 'they are common children you are a lady.' How could I be a 'lady' I was only a child?

It was the year that I had had my fifth birthday when everything began to change; the first change was when father came home dressed in a high ranking officer's uniform and I remember mother crying and saying she wasn't leaving London. On our afternoon walks to the park I noticed the railings had been taken down and a big letter 'S' was being painted on street corners and what excited me most of all were the big balloons that seemed to 'float' over London. I asked nanny, 'why do everyone have to carry funny little boxes? 'Gas masks,' was her reply. Why didn't she ever answer my questions properly; I thought of the gas cooker in the kitchen where Mrs. Peters cooked our meals and began to wonder if I should wear my Mickey Mouse mask in the house in case it exploded.

Nanny and I arrived home one afternoon to find the hall filled with large crates and boxes and the staff busy moving furniture and all our fine china. Mother was darting here and there and giving orders; shouting at the maids to take great care packing her antiques.

Within the week we had left London; I remember crying when I was told that nanny wasn't coming with us as I was old enough now to have a governess and had no need of a nanny as I was a big girl. The governess mother had hired was to travel with us; from the very beginning I disliked her. She was, to me as a child, very old, far older than mother as she had grey hair and wore a grey uniform. Mother had had what father always referred to as 'a tantrum' when father had said that we would travel to Wales by train. After declaring that she had a migraine and a long train journey would upset her nerves and she wasn't going to be seen with the servants who were coming with us; she got her way, as she always seemed to do where father was concerned, and he agreed that we would travel in the Rolls. 'Don't make it any more difficult for me darling Rodney it is hard enough for me, a Lady, to think of travelling to some outlandish place and having to have some country yokel pick us up from a crowded, noisy, dirty train you seem to forget that we are almost royalty.' A few more tears and a lie down in her boudoir with the heavy drapes drawn to shut out the light was enough to make father agree,

I cannot believe how long it took us to drive to Wales as mother kept on insisting at stopping enroute and spending the evening and night in posh hotels. It was exciting for me to stop in these splendid hotels but once in our suite of rooms there I stopped until after breakfast when if mother was, 'up to it' we journeyed on. I cannot say that my governess Miss Fielding was unkind I suppose she was just rather strict.

Mother was getting restless and any little thing I did or any question I asked began to annoy her; so on the third morning father said that as mother had a bad headache it would be a good idea if I sat in front with George our chauffeur so that mother could have peace and quiet.

I really did feel like a 'royal princess'; it was so exciting to see the beautiful country-side in all its autumnal splendour but as we drove through the Welsh valleys the scenery changed it became bleak and a grey smoke and black dust seemed to cover everything. George told me that the black mounds were coal-tips and that the miners dug the coal up from deep down in the earth. Without the coal he had said the trains wouldn't work and all the houses I could see would have no heat and no-where to cook. I couldn't understand why the children I saw playing in the streets looked so dirty and so very raggedy; why were they playing on the road surely they had playrooms in their homes? How misguided I was I had a great deal to learn about the people in the towns and villages where we were to live. Surely now that I was five mother would let me go to a real school I didn't like or want my governess.

Like everything around us the manor house, where father had taken us, looked, for lack of a better word, 'sad'. The gardens were over-grown but I noticed a pretty summer-house and I thought it would make a lovely place to play with my dolls. Beyond the terraced gardens, again very over-grown, were paths that led through wooded areas. The oak and the sycamore had already shed their leaves but the conifers stood tall and erect and at first glance, as we drove up the long drive, I felt it looked 'magical'.

Within a few days of our arrival father took the train back to London as mother insisted that George and the Rolls remained so she could, if she so wished, take herself away from this 'terrible place.' I remember father's words 'Millicent darling you will not be able to use the Rolls as petrol will be in short supply as we will need it all for military use. The Rolls will have to be put up on blocks in the garage.' Another tantrum from mother and instead of seeing him off at the station she took to her bed with a migraine.

I saw very little of mother as she spent her days in the garden room lounging on the chaise longues leaving strict instructions that in no way was she to be disturbed unless she rang the bell.

My mornings were spent with my governess; I was quick to learn and she appeared pleased with my ability; after lunch in the kitchen with Mrs. Peters I was free to wander the grounds and play with my toys. I would take my dolls to the summer house and have a 'tea party' with them. I suppose I got bored with playing the same 'game' and began to wander further into the depths of the garden. Returning one day with my dainty shoes and white socks covered with mud Mrs. Peters said she would see if she could find me some Wellington boots in the village. A new 'adventure' began; wrapped in my warm coat, leggings and fur bonnet I began to 'map' out my secret paths around the immense garden.

Father came home at Christmas and mother became her vibrant, fun loving self; insisting on having visitors for Christmas. Some tuned up in their big cars and those that travelled 1st class by train were picked up at the station by George. Extra staff were brought in from the village and beds were quickly made-up and mother had insisted that her society friends bring some tasty treat with them, chocolates, cake or wine and father had arranged for a large hampers to be sent from Harrods. This all sounds very lavish but I saw very little of the guests or tasted any of the delicacies. My Christmas lunch was in the kitchen with Mrs. Peters, my governess and George; I saw the waitresses coming and going one very pretty lady about mother's age whispered in my ear; 'you should come and play with my Giles we only live around the corner.' 'Around the corner', was another world to me as since our arrival I hadn't been outside the gates to our home. She had set my mind in motion and a plan began to form; surely with all the visitors and lively chatter and music playing on the gramophone I wouldn't be missed. So on

Boxing Day when my parents and most of the guests had gone to The Hunt I quickly ran down one of my 'secret paths' that I knew would lead to the big gates; I looked around and could see no-one and luckily the gates were open and boldly I walked through them. The road was narrow and in the distance I could see the snow-capped mountain tops. I tied my scarf tightly around my neck and keeping to the wall of our estate I continued on my adventure. What had that nice lady said? 'Just around the corner.' Sure enough as I rounded the corner I saw children playing in the street. There must have been about six of them; girls and boys. I was suddenly frightened what had mother said? 'They were 'common'; I didn't understand.' They looked rather shabby but they were all so happy and seemed to be having such fun. 'Come and play,' said one little boy, 'my name is Giles; what is your name?' Before I had time to reply I felt a heavy hand on my shoulder; 'What do you think you are up too young lady? Your mother will be most upset.' It was George the chauffeur and now general 'dog's body' as he referred to himself. I was severely reprimanded by my father and forbidden to leave the house; even to wander in the garden.

Father and the guests returned to London and mother to her bed. It must have been about a month into the New Year that I was summoned to my mother's boudoir. She was dressed in her fine clothes and I noticed a large trunk

and numerous cases and hat boxes were stacked on the landing. I can't describe how excited I was; 'Mother, mother are we going back to London?'
'Please don't shout you sound like a common street urchin and you will give me a headache. No Lydia; I am going back to London to be with your father you, for safety sake, are to stay here and father's cousin Josephine is coming to stay with you as she has no attachments.'
What did 'no attachments' mean?

Mother left and Cousin Josephine moved in; she must have been well over fifty; tall, skinny, gaunt looking; grey hair worn in a chignon and rimless glasses perched on the end of her nose. Under her supervision my lesson took place from ten in the morning with a short break for lunch and then continued until three; every day I was expected to have afternoon tea with her when she would quiz me on my lessons learnt. From Mrs. Peters I began to understand what 'no attachments' meant as I overheard a conversation she had had with one of the maids; 'Quite easy to see why she is an 'old maid' who would ever consider marrying her.' There was a large map in my schoolroom that cousin Josephine had insisted putting up and on it my governess and I had to plot the course the war was taking as it escalated world-wide. Winter turned into spring and the woodland gardens of my home became an overgrown garden of beautiful flowers. I tried to spend more and more time out of doors and even asked Cousin Josephine if we could employ a gardener. I was surprised when she agreed; she said that there were men in the village who would be glad of the job. I thought that perhaps a young man would have been employed so when I first met Henry I was really surprised as to me he was a very old man but I found him amiable and very kind and when I tried to help him with the weeding he encouraged me and soon found other tasks for me to do. The clearing of the over grown woodland brought to light new paths that had been hidden from me one such path ambled up a gentle slope and by following this I found I could just about look over the wall into a garden beyond; this was the day when my lonely existence changed for-ever.

I saw sitting on an upturned pail nursing a chicken was the young boy who had spoken to me when I had 'escaped' on Boxing Day. 'Hello Giles,' I called.
'How did you get up there? Mother told me all about you and said your name is Lydia. Can you climb over the wall?' He put the hen down and crossed towards the wall. 'It is quite low this side; can you find a foot-hole in the loose stones?'
I looked and sure enough there were many such holes; I was at an age where nothing frightened me; so one foot in one hole then the other into one higher and after the third step up I was on top of the wall and then I jumped

down into Giles' back garden.

'Come and help me look for eggs; mother said she thinks one of the hens is broody and laying her eggs somewhere in the garden,'

This was really good fun; forgotten by me that I had on a pair of my best black patent shoes as I walked in chicken droppings and got stung my nettles as we searched for eggs; how chuffed I was to be the one to find a clutch of six eggs hidden under the brambles.

'Come on; let's take these to mother I am sure she will let you stay for tea.'

I didn't have the heart to tell him I had had tea at three o'clock. My, Oh! What a difference tea was in this happy home. I had seen pictures in my story books but this was real I was in a 'real home'.

Giles' mother asked no questions and soon I was sitting down by the kitchen table with a huge 'doorstep' of home-made bread and two boiled eggs.

'Do you like soldiers with your egg?' asked Giles'

'Soldiers,' I quizzed.

'Mother will cut your bread into soldiers to dip in your egg.' It was on this day that I had my first cup of tea; afternoon tea with cousin Josephine were very thin sandwiches and tiny little cakes and my drink was milk.

'Come and meet my friends,' said Giles after I had finished a second piece of home-made cake.

'Perhaps Lydia had better get home before she is missed; come again soon,' said his mother and gave me a hug and

a kiss. Why didn't mother ever hug me like that; I began to feel that perhaps it was because she didn't love me.
Giles helped me back over the wall and shouted after me; 'wear old clothes and wellies next time.'
'Old clothes', I thought; I didn't have any 'old clothes'.
Usually on week-ends I 'escaped' over the wall as Giles had told me that he was in school during the week. How I wished I could go to the village school with Giles and the other children I soon got to know. At first the girls were rather 'shy' of me; Giles told me it was because I had such pretty dresses. One Saturday I had a surprise Giles' mother had bought me a dress and some daps in a jumble sale; after that every time I visited I changed into my 'play clothes'. I learnt to kick a football, to play skipping with the girls and hop-scotch. Cousin Josephine often asked how I had bruised my legs; my explanation was helping Henry in the garden.

In 1944 my life changed completely. A messenger arrived with a telegram for Cousin Josephine; I saw her crumple it up and flee from the room in tears. Picking it up I saw the words that had made Josephine cry: Lord and Lady Huston died instantly when a bomb exploded on the restaurant where they were dining. I ran to Mrs. Peters who for the first time ever hugged me close; 'you poor little rich girl,' she sobbed.
'They', whoever 'they' were thought it wise not for me to

go to London for the funeral and decided that I continue living in the Welsh Valley until the war was over.

I hadn't seen Giles for a few weeks and when I did he gave me a big hug and held my hand. It puzzled me a little that he seemed to know more about my parent's death than I did.

'It was in the papers,' he said, 'it made the headlines as your father was such an important man. It mentioned you and said that you were now a very wealthy young woman.'

'But Giles, I am only a girl how can I be wealthy?'

'Don't you realize that all you need do is ask and everything you want can be yours.'

'So if I asked for a bike for you they would have to give it to me.'

'Don't think they would let you do that,'

I thought I would put my new found knowledge to the test and going to Cousin Josephine I surprised myself with my courage.

'Josephine,' I said, 'I would like you to send to Harrods for two bicycles one for myself and one for my friend.'

All she said was; 'I wondered where you went on the week-end.'

Within a few weeks the bicycles arrived. A blue one for Giles and a red one for me.

No longer was I restricted to the four walls of the garden but when I did go to play I had to tell Cousin Josephine where I was going.

Those summer months were idyllic; we rode the country lanes; ate our sandwiches and drunk our lemonade on the banks of the river where we also slipped off our shoes and socks and paddled in a sparkling, azure blue pool. We laughed and talked and discussed all sorts of things especially what we intended to be when we grew up.

'I want to be a teacher,' said Giles, 'and teach History.

'If you want to be a teacher then so do I and I will teach Geography.'

This was what freedom was all about; we hid from one another in the dense ferns; rolled down the grassy slopes and had such great fun.

'I am going to the Grammar School in September,' said Giles. Mother is so proud of me and has written to father to tell him I passed the entrance exam with flying colours.'

'Can I sit this exam;' I asked.

'I don't know,' was his reply; 'you have always been tutored at home.'

It was then that I made up my mind to tell my governess that now I was ten I wanted to go to the village school as I wanted to sit the exam to go to the Grammar School.

Giles being a year older than me did not deter me from wanting to be in the same school.

How easy I found it was to get my own way so that September I joined the children going to the Junior School. Some I already knew as Giles' friends. I soon found I was far advanced to most of the children in my class. I didn't see quite so much of Giles but he did try to keep most Sundays free for me.

Heavy snows fell that winter and there were days when the school was closed but still I continued to study hard and was glad of my governess' help.

Spring came with all its beauty and then my eleventh birthday that I spent with Giles. It was on this day that I had my first real kiss. We had ridden our bikes up a mountain path that over-looked the village and we were lying in the long, lush grass beside a mountain stream.

'Lydia shall we always remember this day and even if we are ever separated we will meet back here mid-day on your twenty-first birthday. I have saved my pennies from helping mum and have bought you a present.' He handed me a little box and on opening it I found a small brooch in the form of a 'L' for Lydia.

'I love it; it is the best present I have ever had,' and I kissed him lightly on the cheek. 'Thank you so much I will treasure it.'

He put his arms around me and kissed me on the lips; then with a look of embarrassment he got up and shouted, 'Race you down the hill.'

I passed the exam for the Grammar School but to my disappointment I never got to go there as with the end of the war Josephine was instructed that it was time I returned to London where I was enrolled in a school for young ladies. It all came about so suddenly and I had very little chance to spend time with Giles. We sat in his mother's parlour and as we said 'goodbye' we both began to cry. 'Don't forget me,' said Giles. 'Mother has heard rumours that it is not a good thing for a rich young lady to been seen in the company of a village lad and it was time it was stopped as we will soon be both teenagers. Was Giles maturing quicker than I? Because that 'goodbye' kiss was so very, very different.

The following summer I asked could we return to Wales for the summer but was told that the house had been rented out and it wasn't possible to visit there. I continued to write to Giles and he to me. It was the year of my seventeenth birthday when Josephine sprung it on me that it was time to be prepared for presentation at Court and to visit a well-known dress designer to discuss my dress for the debutante's ball and the presentation. Most of my friends were full of talk about what they planned to wear and what eligible bachelor they hoped to catch the eye of. I was making other plans I had a lengthy letter from Giles; he had written that he was putting on hold his entrance to Oxford as he was joining the R.A.F to do his two year military service; he had gone on to say that he still wanted to be a teacher but what excited me was the fact that he was to be stationed at Swinderby and wanted to know that before entering the service perhaps we could spend a week-end together. He apologized that he was short of money and could I make the arrangements. I had no hesitation and in plenty of time before the arranged meeting I had informed Giles where I had booked us rooms. Yes, you are reading correctly, I said rooms. However much I longed to see Giles I was a virgin and wanted to remain that way as all too well I knew the consequences of sex before marriage.

I had booked us into a country pub on the banks of the Thames at Oxford nothing too luxurious as I didn't want Giles to feel ill-at-ease. I drove down in my MG sport and registered and then sat in the lounge waiting for Giles would I recognize him?

I was awe struck when I saw this tall, handsome young man crossing the room towards me. Was it on impulse that I ran straight into his arms? The kiss I received was nothing like that farewell kiss all those years ago. To me it was passionate and I must admit I responded.

'Separate rooms,' he laughed, 'don't you trust me?'

'Perhaps I don't trust myself.'

'I always thought you were the prettiest girl I had ever seen and I loved the photo you sent me last Christmas but I cannot believe how you have changed so much since then; you are so beautiful.'

We had lunch sitting outside watching the Thames winding its way to the sea. I couldn't believe that the boy I had left behind was now a young man drinking pints of ale whilst I sipped lemonade.

We walked hand in hand along the riverbank and sat beneath the shade of a weeping willow to me it was more romantic than any of the romantic films I had seen. His kisses were passionate and I was aware of my burning feelings for him; 'this must stop'. I said to myself as I was well aware of where it would end.

'Let us go and look at the colleges you never know but hopefully we both might end up here one day.' Gone was the moment of passion.

We wandered across bridges and gazed in awe at the splendid architecture; Giles was already on the road to Oxford but it would take some hard work on my part to attain my dream.

When I told him that I was to be presented to the King he laughed; 'must write and tell my parents that my girl-friend is meeting royalty.' Was there a hint of sarcasm in his tone?

'Am I really your girl-friend?'

'You know you are; I fell in love with you the first day I saw you;' he laughed, 'do you realize that is over ten years ago. I doubt if they will ever let a humble school master marry the honorable Lady Lydia.' Again I heard the hint of sarcasm.

'I'd give it all up for you as I would rather be a humble school teacher and a master's wife than live in luxury and never find true love.'

I was hungry; but not for food I was hungry for love. I

could feel the warmth of his body next to mine as we sat, after dining, on a bench in the cool evening air. He had his arm around my shoulders and my head was on his shoulder. Gazing up to the sky he said; if I succeed perhaps one day I will fly one of those planes.'
'I thought that you had said you still wanted to be a teacher?' I questioned.
'I don't know any more perhaps the air-force will make a better career.' He kissed me long and passionately.
'Time we went in,' I said as I felt my temperature rising.
The barman had his beady eye on us as we made our way to the stairs; 'have a goodnight you two lovebirds.'
Giles kissed me as I took the key to unlock the door. Why did I say it? I have no answer only that I was in love and being void of any affection for most of my life it was a wonderful feeling and I didn't want it to stop; 'would you like a night-cap?'
I didn't have to ask twice; but as soon as the door closed behind us Giles' arms were around me and his passionate kisses began to go further; he pulled by cotton top over my head and fumbled to undo my bra. I made no effort to stop him as he almost carried me to the bed. Soon both of us were void of clothes and our intimacy increased; at the back of my mind I recalled many a conversation I had heard from my school mates and knew exactly where our emotions would lead us if I didn't pull away from him.
'You have been with other girls?' My question put a stop to his erection and his love making.

'No. Why do you ask? Why did you stop me have you been with other men?'
'No;' I shouted at him I am a virgin but you appear very knowledgeable.'
'Learnt it all from books and listening to other lads talk about their conquests.'
'Is that what I am to you; a conquest; will you go bragging to your mates?'
I began to cry; my tears brought about a change of the quarrelsome atmosphere.
'Don't cry Lydia, I love you and I would never hurt you or talk about our relationship. I won't make you pregnant I have come prepared.'
I had read about contraception and safe sex but would it be the same? I was soon to find out as our foreplay became intense; all my inhibitions were lost I did things I never thought possible; I made him moan with pleasure but soon the tables were turned and when he 'broke me in' I almost screamed out but he silenced me with his kisses. We slept in each other's arms only to awaken as the sun rose in the eastern sky to make love that took us on a flight of passion. Forgotten was breakfast as we slept until noon.
'How I long to stay and make love to you all day but I have to get to camp by three. Promise we will meet up soon I will write and let you know as I doubt I will get any leave for a while.'

I watched him stride off along the river bank how I longed to run after him. Before bathing and getting dressed I looked at my naked body in the long mirror; I felt different but didn't look any different. It was rather silly of me but I wanted the world to know I was no longer an innocent virgin. I looked at the rumpled bed and thought of Giles and with every thought of him my boyish breast tingled and my nipples became hard with longing.

It seemed ages before we met again and he was pleased to learn that going against all family protocol I had told Josephine I had no wish to be presented in Court and no desire to do the season and no amount of persuasion on her part would make me change my mind.
We always stayed at the same riverside pub and promised the barman that when we did get married he would be the guest of honour.
I don't know why things didn't turn out as I planned; I never sat the entrance exam for Oxford; I refused to go to 'finishing school' and when Giles decided to stay in the R.A.F. and was sent abroad I broke my heart. We corresponded frequently but I wanted to be with him I wanted to be his wife. When I told him this his reply had hurt me as he said that he wouldn't marry me until he was earning enough to support me without my money. I had a mad impulse to donate it all to charity. I wanted to get away from London and all my socialite friends.

Josephine was getting old and becoming very frail so I suggested that perhaps she would like to move to a care home for elderly ladies of class. The suggestion delighted her. I wasn't to receive my inheritance in full until my twenty-first birthday so to make money to support Josephine I arranged to sell our Park Lane house. Before Josephine and I parted company I asked her what had happened to our valley home. She told me it was still mine but had lain empty for a few years and the estate manager had said it had fallen into disrepair.

I didn't tell Giles of my plans but getting touch with his parents I decided to move back to the valley.

I travelled by train, all being 1st class and sent my belongings on by carrier. I travelled to the village in the local bus; no-one guessing who the very plainly dressed young lady was. The bus stopped just before Giles' parent's house and it was only then that a few eyebrows were raised as to whom was the stranger visiting the 'Rees''

'We've tried to make a few rooms comfortable for you but it is best you sleep downstairs as water has been leaking through many of the bedroom ceilings.'

It was far worse than I had anticipated and there was only one thought on my mind; I had a year to get it refurbished before my twenty-first birthday. I hadn't forgotten our date and I so hoped and prayed that Giles hadn't either. His letters continued to be re-directed to me as I didn't wish him to know what my plans were.

I spent Christmas with his parents and it was the best Christmas I ever had; I did arrange for a hamper from Harrods but did not spend money on lavish presents; these were humble folk and I admired their independence. It was a harsh, cold winter with heavy snowfalls that delayed work; I constantly worried about everything being finished in time.
Luckily by the end of May work was completed; the old house had definitely had a face-lift. Modernized completely even down to the old summer-house.
Had I carried my plans too far? You are not going to believe this but I had arranged a wedding; the church, the reception in 'our' new home and even the honeymoon. My money still pulled strings and Giles' 'big chief' was the son of an old friend of the family. Giles was due home on a long awaited leave but I had arranged with his superior for an extended leave for Giles with the promise that he would never know. His parent knew that he was coming on leave but not that I had arranged to extention. They also knew of the wedding plans but what if Giles didn't keep that tryst we made so many years ago to meet on the mountain side overlooking the valley on my 21st birthday.
I was a bag of nerves all my plans had taken shape but what if Giles didn't keep the pre-arranged appointment; what if he didn't wish to marry me? What if he had fallen

in love with someone else? That was a stupid thought as his letters were full of his love for me.

Giles' mother had pretended that she was going shopping and visited me on the day Giles returned home. 'I couldn't believe it was my son when he arrived on the mid-day bus. He is so tall and handsome and not the scrawny lad who last came home before going abroad.'
I was happy that he was home but scared that everything would go wrong. I told his mother of my fears.
'I know my son; he will never break a promise never mind how long ago it was made.'
I spent a restless night and rose early; I put on a pretty white cotton blouse and a fashionable flowered print circular skirt, I tied my hair up in a pony-tail and put on a pair of flat pumps. I felt like a teenager and I suppose I must have looked like one. I pinned to my blouse the brooch with my initial he had given me so many years ago. I set off early; would I be able to hide from him in the long grass? It took me about twenty minutes to reach the spot on the mountain-side, I recalled that last time we had ridden our bikes; very little had changed. I could see for miles and my eyes searched the little white road that would carry my lover to me and five minutes to the hour I saw him turning the bend in the lane. I lay flat down in the long grass and began to count the seconds until we would be reunited: one, two, three, four and so I

continued I had just reached sixty when I could feel him close.

'Lydia,' I heard him call and then he muttered, 'why aren't you here?' I felt him moving closer and then his shadow fell over me.

'Lydia my love you are here, you remembered,'

He fell on his knees beside me and before I had time his lips were upon mine; hungry and demanding; my blouse was soon discarded and had it been the wanton in me that I hadn't worn any underclothes. He caressed and kissed my breasts and then his hands reached under my skirt; there was no time for foreplay he was on top of me and forgotten was the thought of 'being careful'. Lovemaking had been great before but this time it took me to the heights I never wanted to return from; spent of all his emotions he lay beside me in the long grass and together we watched the fluffy white clouds chase each other across the sky.

At last he spoke; raising himself up on one elbow he looked down on me; 'Lydia my love I have been a fool; how I wish I had married you and taken you to Germany with me. Will you marry me?'

'I have waited so long to hear those words. Yes, yes I will marry you.'

'I don't know when I will get the next leave I was only expecting a fortnight this time but was told I had back leave due to me so I wonder if it can be arranged while I am home by special licence.'

I tried hard not to giggle like a school-girl when I said, 'How about Saturday?'

'Stop kidding we'll never get a licence in three days.'

Forgotten was the talk about a wedding as his kisses turned me on and I pulled him down upon me; 'make mad passionate love to me,' I whispered. There was no need to ask him twice.

We lay relaxed and content in each other's arms until the sun disappeared behind a cloud. I reached for my blouse and as I put it on he noticed the brooch. 'You still have it and you wore it today for me.'

'There isn't a day gone by that I haven't gazed upon it and thought of you as it has always been on my dressing table.'

'Race you down the hill,' he shouted as he ran off in front of me. On reaching the bottom he was sitting on a bench waiting for me. 'Where are you staying? He questioned.

'Tell you later.'

'What did you mean by getting married on Saturday surely you are kidding?'

'Let's go and tell your parents our good news,' was the only reply I gave.

'I see some-one has renovated the Manor.'

I said nothing; but over tea set in his mother's parlour all was revealed. 'I have proposed to Lydia and she has accepted me we plan to marry on my next leave,'

'I might be heavily pregnant by then,' I whispered in his ear.

'Hope you brought your dress uniform home,' said his father, 'you are going to need it.'

'Not this time dad I said we will get married on my next leave.'

'Your mother will be disappointed she's bought a new dress and hat and hoped to wear it on Saturday.'

Giles looked at me; 'come on spit it out what is going on and what is all this talk about a wedding on Saturday?'

'Another cup of tea Giles,' said his mother stifling a laugh. 'Shall I tell him Lydia?'

I nodded.

'We hoped you would remember the tryst you two made all those years ago and we hoped and prayed that once you saw Lydia you would propose; I for one know how much you love her as your letters home have only been about Lydia. So your father and I went along with Lydia's plan and what a fun time we've had. The church has been booked, the bans called and the reception prepared but the venue is to be kept a secret; I have my dress and father a new suit; mind you father was loath to spend his hard earned pennies. The bride has her dress all that is left for you to do is to go and buy two wedding bands. The guest list has been sent out; even down to your best man. You needed a push my son and we've given you a big one.'

I waited for his reaction and it wasn't long in coming;

'you little minx I certainly did need a push but what if I hadn't had leave,' He then roared with laughter. 'It won't be worth me arranging married quarters as I told the Big Chief I'm opting out; I have been doing some tutoring for the last two years and I now know I still want to be a teacher. I'll walk with you to the bus stop.'

'No need,' said his father, 'I'm off to the pub. You sit and have a good chat with your mother she has been waiting for the day of your home-coming.'

A special guest of mine had arrived that afternoon and Mrs. Peters had been duly returned to her post as cook. As a child I had thought she was 'old' but when I looked her up to see if she wanted her position back I found that she was only in her fifties and although always referred to as Mrs. Peters she had never been married and was only too eager to return. I had asked her to be my maid-of-honour; she had first declined saying that she was too old and too fat but when I told her I had reached the age of twenty-one without ever having any close friends she said that she would be honoured.

Giles' mother turned up the next day in quite a tizzy as Giles wanted to see me and wanted to know the hotel where I was staying.

On the Friday a few more guests arrived but all in all it was going to be a quiet wedding; or so I thought.

Saturday morning showed every sign that it was going to be one of those glorious, halcyon days of summer. Old George turned up late the previous evening with the Rolls; rented this time. Mrs. Peters helped me to dress and shed tears as she pinned my veil in place with a beautiful diamond tiara just one of the family heirlooms that I had arranged to be taken from the bank where all were put for safe keeping.

Hoping that Giles was safely at the village Church we left at almost noon as it would only take minutes to get to the Church. Small children ran beside the car shouting for pennies; George threw out a handful as was the custom; on arriving at the Church I was amazed to see that it looked as if the whole village had turned out for the wedding. I haven't mentioned my mysterious guest; my guest of honour, who was now sitting beside me in the car and had the honour to 'give me away'. I had kept my promise and had asked Bertie Rogers the barman from our favourite inn, where we had spent many a happy day, to do that honour. The Church bells rang out loud and clear and Mrs. Peters, she had asked me to call her Maud but she had always been Mrs. Peters and would remain so, was waiting at the Church door with the Vicar. I walked into the cool, ancient building and the sun streamed in through the stained glass windows and the rays shone on Giles stand resplendent in his uniform waiting for me. I saw a smile creep across his face; I don't think it was for me but for my entourage.

Slowly I walked down the aisle as the organist played the Bridal March; as I arrived by his side he whispered, 'I love you.'

Vows, hymns, blessings and bible reading all went over my head except for the words; 'I now declare you husband and wife. I was Mrs. Giles Rees and happy was the bride that the sun shone on that day.

Together we walked back down the aisle and out into the sunshine; the smell of the orange blossom tree that grew in the church-yard filling the air. Then we both stood agape as standing making a guard of honour were old friends from his first air-force base; something his best-man had arranged without our knowledge. Photographs taken we made for the car that would take us to our reception. Again Giles saw the humorous side when he saw George seated in the Rolls. 'Didn't know you still had the old car.'

'Not mine, rented for the day.' I didn't tell him until later that George was going to make his home with us as odd job man; if I had it would have given the game away.

'Is the reception at your hotel?' I didn't answer as I had already instructed George to drive around town to give the guests time to get back to the Manor.

'Almost forgot,' said Giles as he delved into his pocket, 'I have a present for you; think it should have come first.'

He opened a small box and took from it a beautiful three stoned diamond engagement ring and slipped it on my finger above my beautiful wedding band. 'Do you know, my love I am beginning to get suspicious? George has driven twice around the town and where we are now I know there are no hotels that would be suitable for you to hold our reception'.
I opened the sliding window and said; 'Home George.'
'Home?' questioned Giles. 'There is no way mother is putting on the reception. Come on 'spit it out'.'

As we drove slowly through the village the youngsters again ran by the side of the car. George stopped the car and handed out sweets and pennies to the children who ran off in delight.
We passed the last house in the village, his old home and rounding the bend in the road I could see Giles' face light up. 'I noticed that it had been done up but mother hadn't told me it was a hotel that catered for weddings.'
We drove in through the open gates; very shiny and very new and up the gravel drive and standing on the terrace were our guests. It was Mrs. Peters who let the 'cat out of the bag.'
'Welcome to your new home Mr. and Mrs. Rees.'
'Our new home,' repeated Giles and picking me up in his arms he carried me over the threshold. 'I'll sort you out later.'
'Can't wait,' was my reply.

Even if I say it myself the day was perfect; the food delicious and wine and champagne flowed freely.

I went to change into my going away outfit; it was a Chanel suit in the palest of lilac and it had cost me the earth but it was my day and I wanted to look just perfect and navy accessories completed my ensemble.

George was waiting in the Rolls and we left our new home in a shower of confetti and hugs and kisses.

'Where are we off to now? Are you sure you haven't joined the Secret Service?'

'To the airport.'

Then where?

'Paris, Rome, New York where would you like to go?'

'Paris is the city for lovers so what about Paris?'

'Your wish has been granted.'

'Can I have three wishes please?'

'What are your other wishes Giles?'

'I wish for a long and happy life with you my beautiful wife and my third wish is for four beautiful children and that my daughters will look just like their very beautiful mother.'

'And our sons like their handsome father,' I whispered.'

I will end my story now as our honeymoon was just for us; I will tell you though that Paris was beautiful and the perfect city for romance and lovers. The moon looked larger and cast its reflection on the river; the starlit sky a deeper shade of midnight blue; God was in his heaven and all was right with the world.

There is one other thing that I know you are longing to know; our lovemaking in the long grass resulted in the birth of our son nine months to the day of our wedding. We named him Jonathan; I made a vow then that no garden wall would keep my children 'locked away' from the children of the village or village life.

NB:- All peoples' names are fictitious

In Flanders' Fields

In Flanders' fields the poppies blow
Between the crosses row on row,
That mark our place and in the sky
The larks, still bravely singing fly
Scarce heard amid the guns below.

We are the dead. Short days ago
We lived, felt dawn, saw sunset glow,
Loved and were loved and now we lie
In Flanders' Field

Take up your quarrel with the foe;
To you from failing hands we throw
The torch, be yours to hold on high.
If you break faith with us who die
We shall not sleep. Though poppies grow
In Flanders' Field

Major John McCrae 1915

Lest we Forget

They shall not grow old
As we that are left grow old
Age shall not weary them
Nor the years condemn
At the going down of the sun
And in the morning
We will remember them.

Ecclesiastes Chapter 3 verses 1 – 8

To everything turn; turn; turn
There is a Season; turn; turn; turn
And a time to every purpose under heaven.
A time to be born; A time to die;

A time to plant; A time to reap;
A time to kill; A time to heal;
A time to love; A time to weep.

To everything; turn; turn; turn
There is a Season; turn; turn; turn:
And a time for every purpose under heaven.
A time to build up; A time to break down:
A time to dance; A time to mourn:
A time to cast away stones; A time to gather stones together.

To everything turn; turn; turn:
There is a Season; turn; turn; turn:
And a time to every purpose under heaven.
A time of love; A time of hate.
A time of war; A time of peace.
A time you may embrace; A time to refrain from embracing.

To everything turn; turn; turn.
There is a Season; turn; turn; turn.
And a time for every purpose under heaven.
A time to gain; A time to lose.
A time to rend; A time to sew.
A time to love; A time to hate.
A time of peace; I swear it's not too late.

To everything turn; turn; turn.
There is a Season; turn; turn; turn.
And a time for every purpose under heaven.
To everything turn; turn; turn.
There is a Season; turn; turn; turn.
And a time for every purpose under heaven.

Alchemy of a Woman

In the original Sanskrit, the creation of woman by Twashtri, the Vulcan of Hindu mythology, is described thus:
"He took the lightness of the leaf and the glance of the fawn, the gaiety of the sun's rays and the tears of the mist, the inconstancy of the wind and the timidity of the hare, the vanity of the peacock and the softness of the down on the throat of the swallow. He added the harshness of the diamond, the sweet flavour of honey, the cruelty of the tiger, the warmth of fire and the chill of snow. He added the chatter of the jay and the cooing of the turtle dove. He melted all this and formed a woman. Then he made a present of her to man."

1 Corinthians 13 King James Version

Though I speak with the tongues of men and of angels and have not charity I am become as sounding brass or a tinkling cymbal. And though I have the gift of prophecy and understand all mysteries and all knowledge, and though I have all faith, so that I could remove mountains and have not charity, I am nothing. And though I bestow all my goods to feed the poor, and though I give my body to be burned and have not charity, it profiteth me nothing. Charity suffereth long and is kind, charity envieth not, charity vaunteth not itself, is not puffed up. Doth not behave itself unseemly, seeketh not her own, is not easily provoked, thinketh no evil. Rejoiceth not in iniquity, but rejoiceth in the truth. Beareth all things, believeth all things, hopeth all things, endureth all things. Charity never faileth, but whether there be prophecies, they shall fail, whether there be tongues, they shall cease, whether there be knowledge, it shall vanish away. When I was a child, I spake as a child, I understood as a child, I thought as a child but when I became a man, I put away childish things. For now we see through a glass, darkly; but then face to face, now I know in part but then shall I know even as also I am known. And now abideth faith, hope, charity, these three, but the greatest of these is charity.

The Gate of the Year

And I said to the man who stood at the gate of the year:
"Give me a light, that I my tread softly into the unknown!"
And he replied:
"Go out into the darkness and put your hand into the Hand of God.
That shall be to you better than light and safer than the known way."
So, I went forth, and finding the Hand of God, trod gladly into the night
And he led me towards the hills and the breaking of day in the lone East.
So heart, be still
What need our little life,
Our human life, to know,
If God hath comprehension?
In all the dizzy strife
Of things both high and low
God hideth his intention.

The Desert 1908 – Marie Louise Haskins 1876-1957
This poem was quoted by King George V1 Christmas 1939

Footprints Prayer
Footprints in the Sand

One night I had a dream…
I dreamed I was walking along the beach with the Lord a
And across the sky flashed scenes from my life
For each scene I noticed two sets of footprints in the sand,
One belonging to me, and the other to the Lord.
When the last scene of my life flashed before us,
I looked back at the footprints in the sand.
I noticed that many times along the path of my life,
There was only one set of footprints.
I also noticed that it happened at the very lowest and saddest times of my life
This really bothered me, and I questioned the Lord about it.
"Lord you said that once I decided to follow you,
You would walk with me all the way,
But I have noticed that during the most troublesome times in my life,
There is only one set of footprints.
I don't understand why in times when I
Needed you the most, you should leave me."
The Lord replied, "My precious, precious
Child I love you, and I would never,

Never leave you during your times of
Trial and suffering.
When you saw only one set of footprints
It was then that I carried you."

Morte D'Arthur

And slowly answered Arthur from the barge;
"The old order changeth, yielding place to new,
And God fulfils himself in many different ways,
Lest one good custom should corrupt the world.
Comfort thyself, what comfort is in me?
I have lived my life, and that which I have done
May he within himself make pure! But thou
If thou shouldst never see my face again
Pray for my soul. More things are wrought by prayer
Than this world dreams of; wherefore, let thy voice
Rise like a fountain for me night and day
For what are men better than sheep or goats
That nourish a blind life within the brain
If knowing God they lift not hands of prayer
Both for themselves and those who call them friend?
So said he, and the barge with oar and sail
Moved from the brink, like one full-breasted swan,
That fluting a wild carol ere his death
Ruffles her pure, cold plume,
and takes to flood with swarthy webs.

By Alfred - Lord Tennyson

Polonius' Advice to his Son

Give thy thoughts no tongue,
Nor unproportion'd thought his act.
Be thou familiar, but by no means vulgar,
Those friends thou hast, and their adoption tried,
Grapple them to your soul with hoops of steel;
But do not dull thy palm with entertainment
Of each new hatch'd, unfledged comrade. Beware
Of entrance to a quarrel, but being in,
Bear't that the opposed may beware of thee.
Give every man thy ear, but few thy voice;
Take each man's censure, but reserve thy judgment.
Costly thy habit as thy purse can buy.
But not express'd in fancy; rich, not gaudy;
For the apparel oft proclaims the man.
Neither a borrower or lender be;
For loan oft loses both itself and friend,
And borrowing dulls the edge of husbandry.
This above all; to thine ownself be true,
And it must follow, as the night the day,
Thou canst not then be false to any man.

By William Shakespeare (1564-1616)

Mercy

From: A Merchant of Venice
By William Shakespeare

The quality of mercy is not strain'd,
It droppeth as the gentle rain from heaven
Upon the place beneath: It is twice blest;
It blesses him that gives and him that takes,
'Tis mightiest in the mightiest; it becomes
The throned monarch better than his crown;
His scepter shows the force of temporal power,
The attribute to awe and majesty,
Wherin doth sit the dread and fear of kings;
But mercy is above the sceptered sway;
It is enthroned in the hearts of kings,
It is attribute to God himself;
And earthly power doth show likest God
When mercy seasons justice.

Yours

The life that I have
Is all that I have
And the life that I have is yours.
The love that I have
Of the life that I have
Is yours, and yours and yours.
A sleep I shall have
A rest I shall have
Yet death will be but a pause.
For the peace of my years
In the long green grass
Will be yours, and yours and yours.

By Leo Marks
Made famous by the 1958 film
'Carve Her Name with Pride'

Unchained Melody
Lyrics by Hy Zaret

Oh! My love, my darling,
I've hungered for your touch
A long lonely time.
And time goes by so slowly
And time can do so much
Are you still mine?
I need your love
Oh! I need your love
God speed your love to me.
Lonely rivers flow to the sea,
To the sea; to the open arms of the sea
Lonely rivers sigh, wait for me, wait for me
I'll be coming home, wait for me.

'Mammy Val's Little Book of Allsorts'

Union Songs
Bells of Rhymney
Words by Idris Davies
Set to music by Pete Seeger

Oh! What will you give me?
Say the sad bells of Rhymney
Is there hope for the future?
Cry the bells of Merthyr
Who made the mine owner?
Say the black bells of Rhondda
And robbed the miner
Cry the grim bells of Blaina

They will plunder willy-nilly
Cry the bells of Caerphilly
They have fangs, they have teeth
Say the loud bells of Neath
Even God is uneasy
Say the moist bells of Swansea
And what will you give me
Say the sad bells of Rhymney.

Put the vandals in court
Say the bells of Newport
All would be well, if, if, if

Cry the green bells of Cardiff
Why so worried sisters, why
Sang the silver bells of Wye
And what will you give me
Say thee sad bells of Rhymney.

A Dog's Last Will and Testament

Before humans die they write their Last Will and
Testament and give their homes and all they have to
those they leave behind.
If with my paws I could do the same this is what I'd ask
To a poor and lonely Stray I'd give
My happy home
My bowl and cosy bed, soft pillow and all my toys
The lap which I loved so much, the tender loving touch
The hand that stroked my fur and sweet voice that called
my name.
I'd will to the sad, scared Shelter Dog
The place I had in my human's heart
Of which there seemed no bounds.
So when I die please do not say
'I will never have a pet again
For the loss and pain is more than I can stand.'

Instead go find an unloved dog
One whose life held no joy or hope
And give my place to him.
This is the only thing I can give
The love I left behind.

Jerusalem
By William Blake

And did those feet in ancient times,
Walk upon England's mountains green,
And was the Holy Lamb of God
On England's pleasant pastures seen?
And did the Countenance Divine,
Shine forth upon our clouded hills.
And was Jerusalem builded here
Among those dark Satanic mills?
Bring me my bow of burning gold,
Bring me my arrows of desire
Bring my spear, 'O' clouds unfold!'
Bring me chariot of fire.
I will not cease from mental fight
Nor shall my sword sleep in my hand
'Till we have built Jerusalem
In England's green and pleasant land.

Dodie's
Letters Home

Dorothy Lamb (or Dodie as she liked to be called) was evacuated from Brixton London during the last war and came to live with my grandmother and her bachelor brother (the kindest man who replaced my very strict father in my heart and remained there) in the village of Cefn Pennar in the Cynon Valley. My mother and I also returned to The Valley in 1942. How grand-mother coped with her 'full house' when Dorothy's parents visited and also my father. Her parents kept in touch with my grandmother until their death; after which Dorothy kept up the correspondence and came to visit grandmother on her 100th birthday.

After Dodie's untimely death letters that she had written home to her parents on scraps of paper were sent to me and now compiling this 'little book of allsorts' I thought that on 3rd September 2014 it was 75 years since the start of WW2 that they might be of interest. I am unable to print all of them as obviously those written in pencil have faded. A big thank you goes to my friend David Redd for taking time and effort to get them as good as he possibly could. I cannot envisage a child today writing such letters. I suppose there is no need for a child to sit down today and write a letter as it is so easy to send a message on a mobile phone. Is letter writing a dying 'art'? I do hope you will enjoy reading those that I have printed and also find them very 'heartwarming' as one can hardly envisage how stressful it was for the young evacuees leaving their parents and their home. Dodie was one of the 'lucky' ones as she was loved and cared for by my grand-mother and mother. If you would like to read more about my grandmother her life story is for sale on Amazon – 'Gwenllian – her story 1886-1986

Back Row: Jean Hughes: Sheila Bennett: Maureen Lewis Front Row: Dorothy Lamb and Jessie Barnbrook (another evacuee)

Dear mummy
and daddy
I am quite
well and
happy
thank you
for parcel
love from Dorthy
x x   x x

Parcel arrived safely
many thanks. G. Baker
will write soon

'Mammy Val's Little Book of Allsorts'

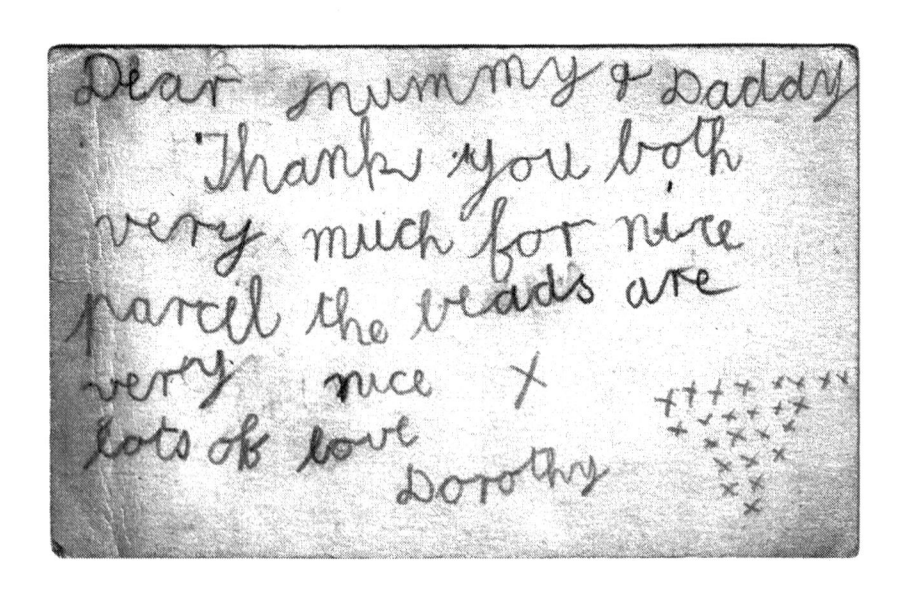

Dear mummy & Daddy
Thank you both very much for nice parcel the beads are very nice x
lots of love
Dorothy

David Redd has tried to put all the following letters in sequence – a hard task.

Dorothy's reference to a visit to gran's niece at Pontypool. The reason my mother and I didn't go was due to the fact that my father was home on a visit. I was quite upset that I couldn't go on the train as I found it amazing how slow the train went over Crumlin Viaduct and I so loved my Auntie Florrie. I was quite pleased to have a present as auntie sent me a little elephant egg-cup (still have it) and grandmother brought back lots of home-made goodies.

Dear mummy & daddy.
I was pleased to have a nice
parcel of sweets, and
thank you for my new
money and letter.
I am very well and
getting on alright at school
I had a nice holiday
with Auntie at ponty-
pool
I enjoyed feeding the
chickens and picking up
the pears and apples the
wind had blown down
on the garden.
give granny my love

26 Greenfield Terrace
Cefnpennar,
Mountain Ash.
Oct 22nd 1942

Dear Mrs Lamb
 I received your last welcome letter & sent the form to school but I have had no more inquiries I hope you are both keeping well & please tell Dorothy's Grannie she received her parcel safely. I have not been very well just lately, and I have been thinking to ask you to have Dorothy home again as I think she need your care she gets off untill dark in the evenings & goes off & get wet feet if I dont happen to put her Wellingtons on up around the fields, well I

dont want you to think I am unkind but really I feel I cannot cope with it during this winter again, she is very well at present, but she just dont bother to listen to anything I say, so please concider the matter & let me know if you can come any time during this next month I know you have been very kind & thoughtful about everything for her welfare & I have done my best for her,

    So please accept my kind regards to you both

    Yours Sincerely
    G. Evans

26 Greenfield Terrace
Cefnpennar
Mountain Ash
April 15th 1943

Dear Dorothy

I must write you a little letter dear thanking you for my birthday card it was very nice of you to remember, Well now its your birthday so I hope you will have a nice time & we all send our best wishes I hope dear you are quite well also Mummy & Daddy we are very well here at present, and what nice weather we are having. Pat Tate asked me the other day about you dear, I am sure she do miss you as you were very good friends. I expect Valerie will have to start school this year, as she will be four in July, and she is growing quite tall. I am sure you are able to help & do lots of work for mums now you are getting a big girl. I received Mums last letter so with kind regards to her & daddy & love to yourself dear From auntie Gwen xx

This is a letter my grand-mother wrote to Dorothy I didn't start school until after my fifth birthday.

Aged four a 'letter' I sent Dorothy

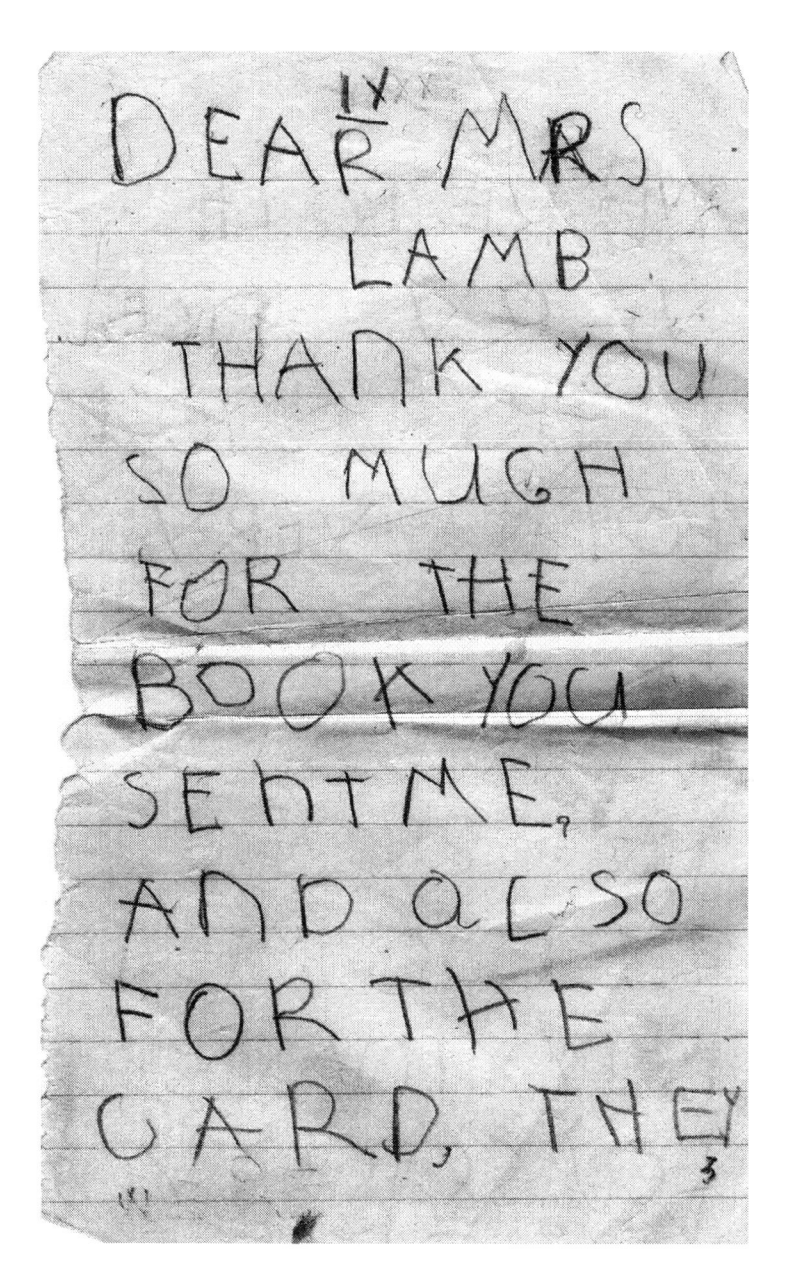

> DEAR MRS LAMB THANK YOU SO MUCH FOR THE BOOK YOU SENT ME, AND ALSO FOR THE CARD, THEY

Aged five a letter I sent to Mrs. Lamb – I still have the book.

2 xx

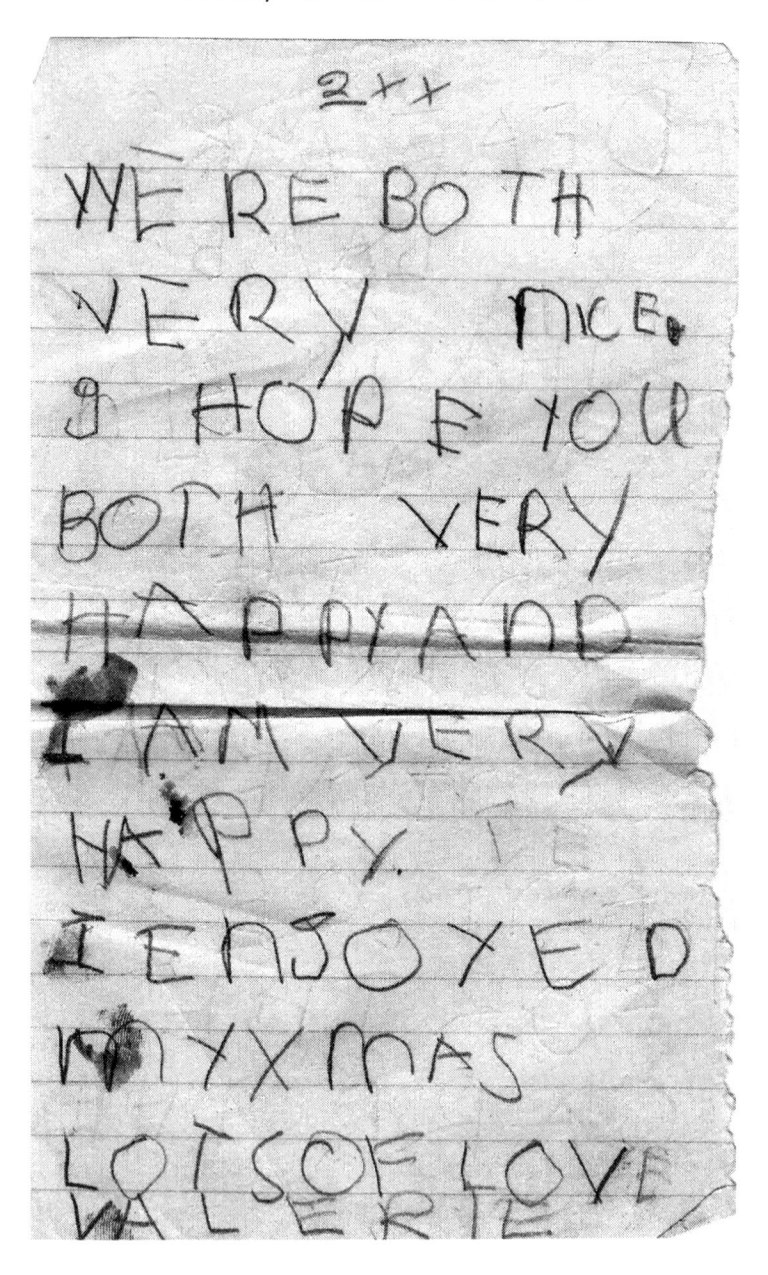

WE'RE BOTH
VERY nice.
I HOPE YOU
BOTH VERY
HAPPY AND
I AM VERY
HAPPY.
I ENJOYED
MY XMAS
LOTS OF LOVE
VALERIE

B19
57 Tnelam
Rd   Brixton
         S.W.2.   June
                              16

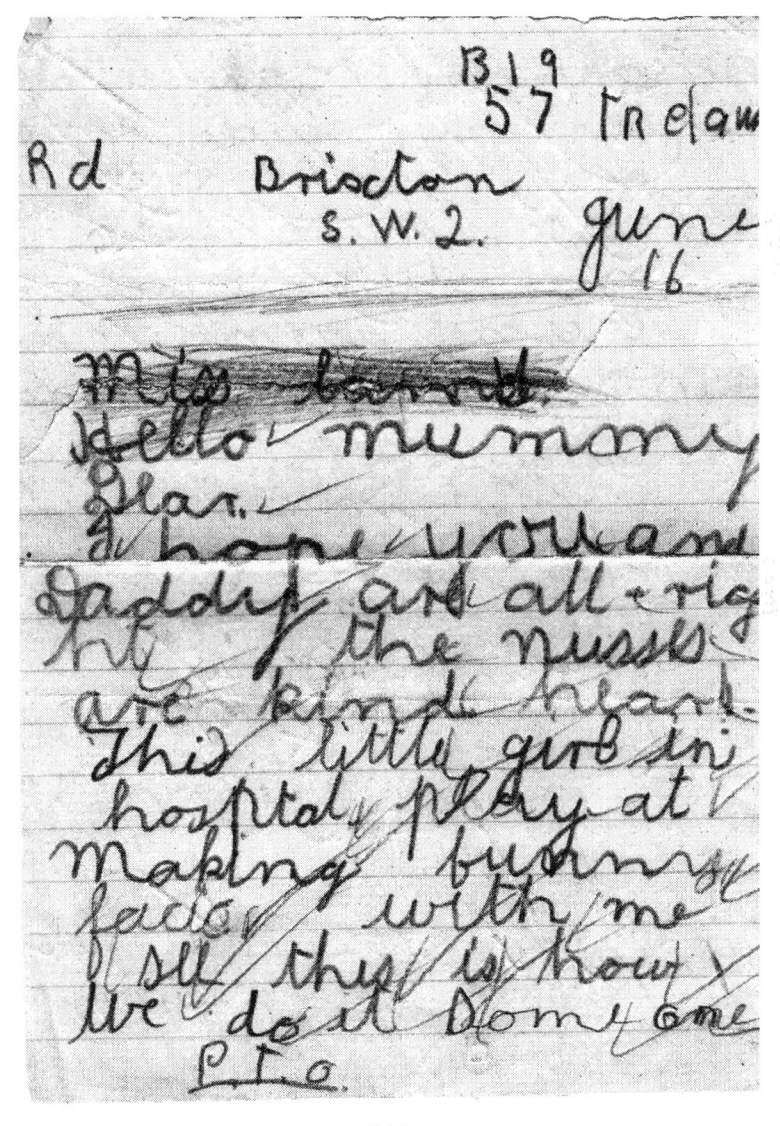

~~Miss ~~
Hello mummy
dear,
I hope you and
Daddy are all-rig
ht. The nusses
are kind hearted
this little girl in
hospital play at
making bunny
faces with me
all this is how
we do it. Nom+ome
    P.T.O.

'Mammy Val's Little Book of Allsorts'

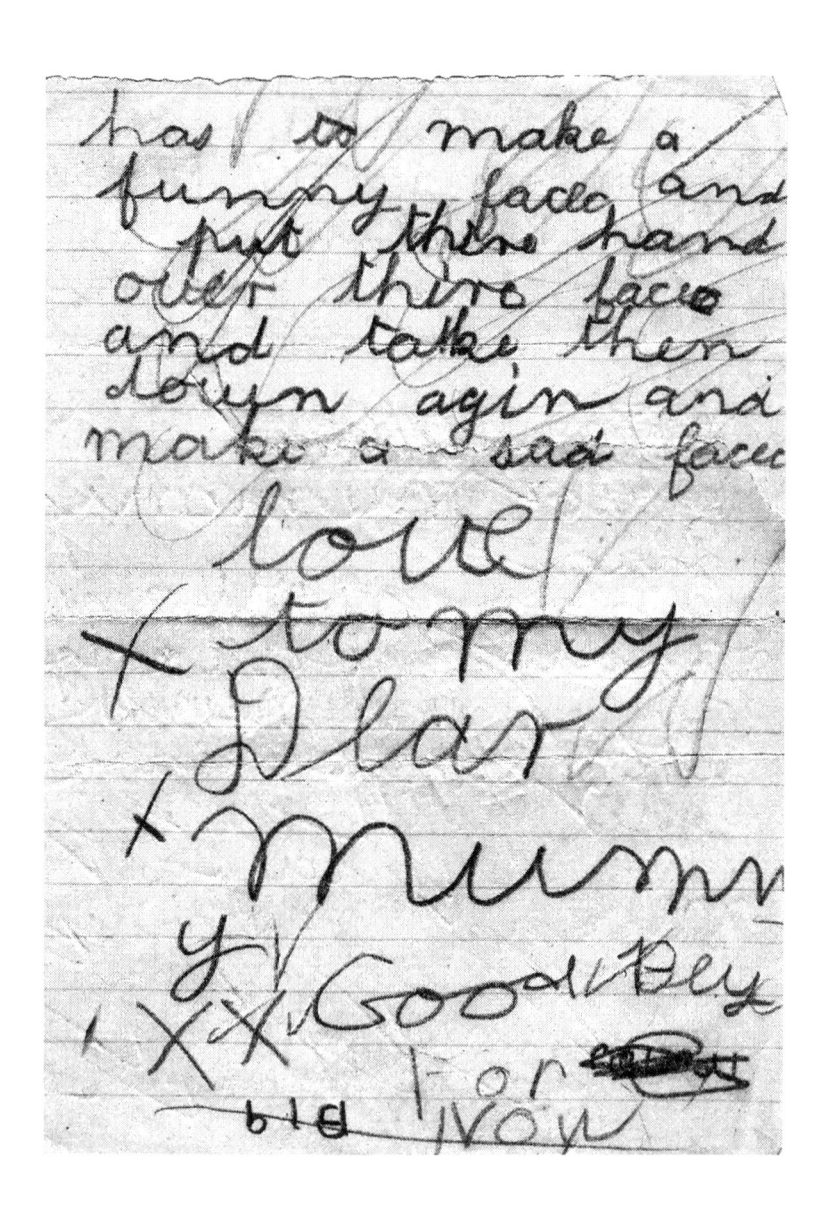

has to make a funny face and put there hand over there face and take then down agin and make a sad face

love to my Dear mum
xxx Goodbey
For Now

P.S.
We recieved the two parcels you sent us. And Auntie thanks you for the swich, and she said she will write soon

x x

'Mammy Val's Little Book of Allsorts'

26 Greenfield Terrace
Cefnpennar
Mountain Ash

Dear Mrs Lamb
　　　　Just a few lines to put in with Dorothy's letter. Have you any warm knickers & liberty bodices for Dorothy she said you had got some if so I would be glad if you sent them on as the weather is getting a bit nippy now. Thanks for your last letter our letters crossed last time, hope you are both fairly well, we are all very well here thanks.
You are still getting those bombs now occasionally so we hear. Hope your mother is a little better, will close now with kind regards to you both
　　　　　　yours G. Evans

Val Baker Addicott

26 Greenfield
Terrace Cotford
Mountain Ash

Dear Mum,
hope you are
alright and
keep keeping fit.
I am alright.
Will you
promise me one
thing when
October comes you
will let me

'Mammy Val's Little Book of Allsorts'

Come home although the war is not over I hope Daddy got home saftly at night or some times when I have nothing to do tears come to my eyes. If you would like to know arrived home saftley. When

Val Baker Addicott

I was in the train there was a RAF girl she was very nice, and she talked to Dad a lot, and when we had been quite a long way she had a little
P.T.O

nap and
she was sleeping
she dribbeled on
daddy. I am
going to school
to-day Wednesday
19th. Oh I
ment to tell
you before as
I was walking
Valerie came
next page

Val Baker Addicott

to met us I 2
did'nt know her
she had grown
so big. I was
saying, is this
valerie, is this
valerie. I am
nearly crying
now, infact I
am now. Come
and see me,
I had an ice-
cream.
P.T.O

'Mammy Val's Little Book of Allsorts'

Well I am sorry to have to close now, Well Good bye. keep very safe From Goldie to my Dear Darling mum my. xxxx xxxxxxx xx xxxxx

Val Baker Addicott

10

R.C. Green
22/7/44

Dear Mum & Dad
 I hope you are alright & happy. I am quite well and happy too. I have been to school for a week & I like it very much, they have put
p.t.o

'Mammy Val's Little Book of Allsorts'

me in Std. 4. I go to Gwm Penny school, Tis a long walk but it is very nice on a fine day. We have a bus if it should Rain. I went to the chapel tea last Thursday. They asked me if I would like to go, as you know

Next Page

Val Baker Addicott

11

I used to go to chapel when I was here before I hope Dad you are better & Mum look after your self & may God take care of you Both. With lots of love from. Dodie.

P.s Give my love to David aunty

x x x x
x x x x
x x x
x

x x
x x

x x x x x
x x x x x
x x x x x
x

'Mammy Val's Little Book of Allsorts'

Dear Mum and Dad, Just a few lines to you. We'll mum I am alright and happy too. I will soon be home again to see you. Valerie is fine now do you no what. I sent
P.T.O

Val Baker Addicott

her a nice V
brouch with
red whit and
blue stripes it
is real silver.
Well, I think
I'o better close
now cause its
time to go to
sleep. Well bye
bye now. Love TO
mum, from Rodie
X X X X V V V V V V V

'Mammy Val's Little Book of Allsorts'

P.S
I Riceved your lovely letter. I went to Mr Friday and auntie phill got some Musta wool and I an starting to knit a bathing-costume for my self, and — — — one to. Well I must close with Love To
P.T.O.

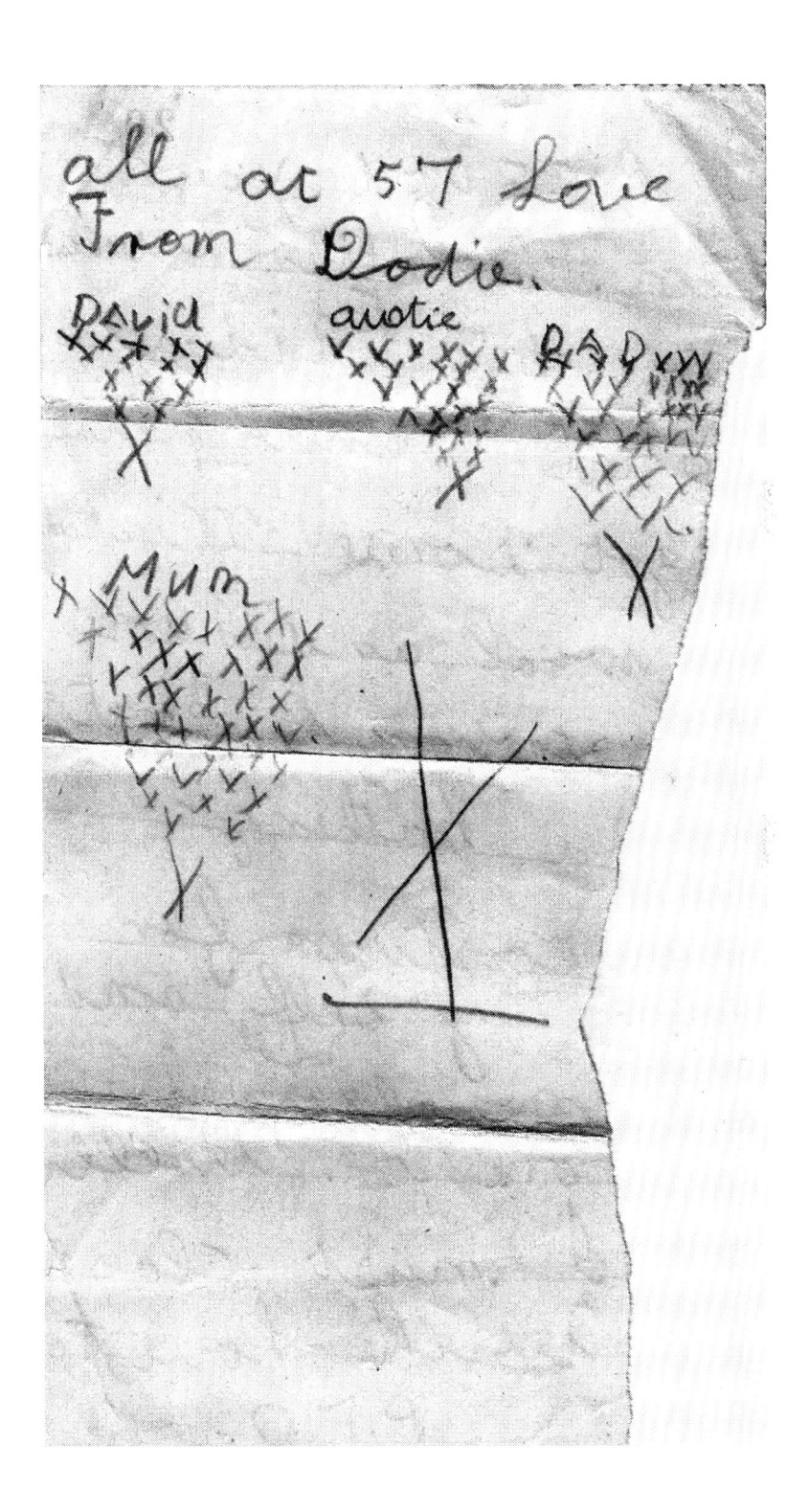

Val Baker Addicott

all at 57 Love
From Dodie
David   auntie   RAD
xxxxx   xxxxxx x   xxx
 xxx   xxxxx   xxx
  x   x   x
                     x

 Mum
xxxxx
xxxxxx
xxxxxx
 xxxx
  xx
   x

'Mammy Val's Little Book of Allsorts'

26 Green Field
Terrace M Tash
20th of Aug

Dear Mum,

Thank you so much for that lovely parcel you sent me, they were very nice. I had another parcel from Grannie. Its been very hot weather since last Friday and it has been raining since

PTO

it has been nasty. We went to the pictures last week. I'm so glad that the news is much brighter, and now the war will soon come to an end. The blackberries are coming out quitely I hope to have a

'Mammy Val's Little Book of Allsorts'

blackberries tart soon. I hope you will soon come down and see me soon. Are you going to send my swim suit down, Auntie Phil has nearly finished my swim suit. You can send it down if you want to. I dont mind. Well now I must say Good-by and God Bless you all. Love to

Val Baker Addicott

Kisses to Auntie xxx
Molly & David vvv

'Mammy Val's Little Book of Allsorts'

Dere Mum & Dad
 Thank you so much for you lovely letter, and also for the stamp. We went to the Harvest festival in chapel down the rnt, a week ago, and last Sunday we went to the festival in Church up, here, it was a lovely service. We all went to Pictures last Friday, it was
P.T.O

Val Baker Addicott

good too. We had half
holiday Friday afternoon
I am making a lot
of clothes for my
doll. I hope you are
all well. Valerie
is worrying about
~~why dont I bring Susy~~
down. I hope Granny
is getting better quickly
Well I must say
good bye and all
keep well Love Dodi

'Mammy Val's Little Book of Allsorts'

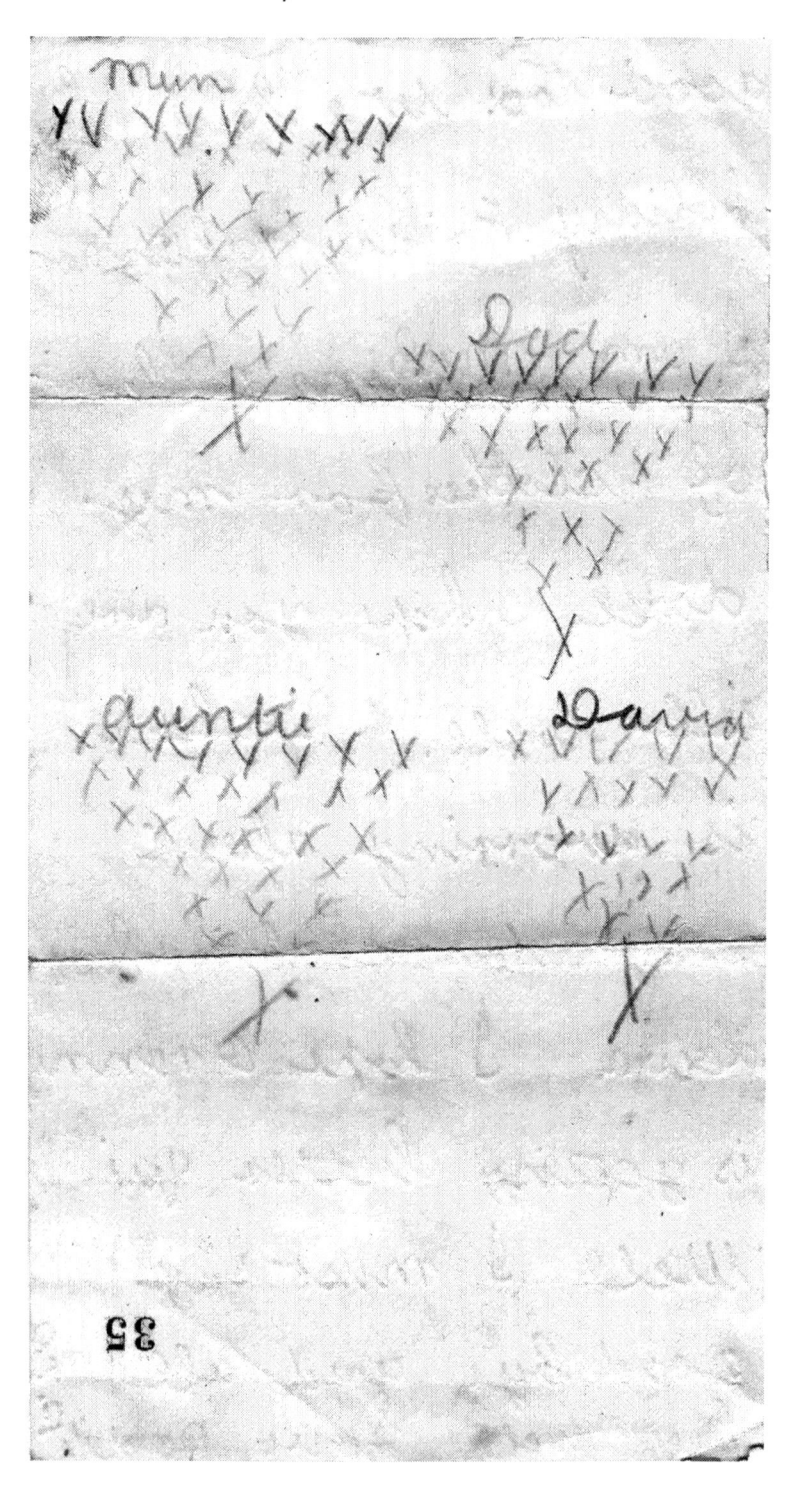

ARE you COMING DOWN HOME ON EASTER

26 Greenfield Terrace
Cefnpennar
Mountain Ash

Dear Mummy & Daddy
I hope you are keeping well, I am keeping very well thank-you. Thank you so much for the lovely letter and also the 2/- it was very nice of you to think of me. Oh! do you know that Mrs. Barnbrook has got another little girl,? I wonderd wheather you would know about it, Maureen's Auntie Esther told Mrs Lewis, and Mrs Lewis told us. Auntie Phyll made me a skirt, it is

PTO

'Mammy Val's Little Book of Allsorts'

Note: The word 'lovely' was on the back of page.

*with love and lots of kisses
From your loving
Daughter
Dorothy
ps
Sylvia gave me some
fishes I have 4 all toge-
togetter*

xxxxxxxxxxxxxxxxx

try this grandma

*Your word is MOTHER
what is mine. xxx*

Val Baker Addicott

26 Green Feild Terr
42
Cefnpenna
Mountain as
Snow
Oct 15th 44

Dear Mum & Dad.
 I hope you are keeping well and happy as I am. I am glad you like that picture the three small girls with Deanna Derbin. I wish I was there to see it. We have we
PTO

'Mammy Val's Little Book of Allsorts'

2xx

in school I don't like it much. There is a new song on the wireless called Swinning on a Star. All the children had dinners in school I asked Auntie could I have them in school Kill at last she let me, they are lovely dinners I enjoyed them. Carol Cor is a lovely singer & Helen Hill. I think Joanne Perkin is better still.

— Note

Note:- the inevitable ink blots on these letters when using pen and ink it was the norm for our exercise books to be covered with blots and also our fingers. Dorothy wrote these letters home to her parents on scraps of paper and even on opened up used envelopes - this information is for those reading these letters who are not aware of paper shortage during WW2. Dorothy refers to my mother (Auntie Phyl) making her a skirt. My mother spent many long hours during the war years sewing for the people of the village; cutting down men's old jackets or top coats and making Churchill type 'boiler suits' for the village lads. I can still recall sitting on the rag mat by her feet picking up the cut off cotton threads and odd bits of material. Nothing was wasted as my grandmother and her brother would sit each side of the fire-place 'pegging' strips of material into an old (washed) sack to make our rag mats; occasionally I helped. Fun to me was to sit there on the rug remembering what my mother had made from each piece.Note – page 217 – the V brooch that Dorothy referred to must have been for Victory – I still have the brooch and always thought that my father had bought it for me; it wasn't until I received these letters after Dorothy's death that I found that it was a gift from Dorothy. There are a lot more letters – perhaps enough to make a book about evacuees from WW2.

'Mammy Val's Little Book of Allsorts'

Did you see Auntie Peg. Who sent me that little box that, that lays in Ireland with all the medals, and my writting book that Uncle Harry sent me. Who sent me that ring and bracelet. I hope I will soon be home again. I have made a little skirt with straps and a piece and a lot of other all for his dol she looks very nice in them Well I must say

Val Baker Addicott

Good bye and
God Protect you
and all of you
Love Dodie
sincerly
Dodie

MUM   DAD
xxxxxxxxx
xxxxxxxxx
xxxxxxx
xxxxx
xxx
X

Love   Love
auntie   DAVID
xxxxxxxyy   xxxxxxA
xxxxxxx   xxxxx

x   love xx

26, Greenfield Terrace
Cefn Pennar
Mountain Ash

Dear Mummy & Daddy,
 I hope you are all right and happy as I am. Thank you so much for the lovely parcel you sent to me, it was very nice of you, for knitting that lovely, lovely, red cardigean and the beautifull shoes they just fit me they <u>are</u> nice. Sylvia Bebb said she would give a book or some dolls cloth just for some fudms stars. I have given her some, I have just got to give a couple more, she asked me what would I

like I said I would like a book so she is going to give me a book. Oh Mam if you see any film stars in any books will you send them, but you needn't hunt all over the place for them, just as you see them in a book or in the papers, if you have any of them film stars in the cigarette cases if you have any to spare send them along because I am saving them. I had this card from Auntie Gladys, she seems a bit cross but I have written her two letters one to thank her for the calendar and one for the Christmas present also I sent her a Christmas card it was so

↙ X   26 Green Feild
       Terrace

       Cefnpennar

       m⁺ ash

                Nov 26th

Dear Mum and Dad
I hope you are
alright and happy
as I am. Thank you
so much for the
parcel you sent me.
Auntie thanks
you for the things
you sent her. I
am longing to come
home and see you all

again, I hope the war will soon be over, we had to write a composition on "After the war I put, "We would have pink ice-cream and then white ice-cream and cherries on top." Do you know we can have ice-cream? I dont mean the blocks of ice we had before this is the real ice-cream but it is not the prewar, Some people do say, "We will have the real thing on the tenth of next month." You can send me what you like, dont send me a lot of things because you wont have the money. I just asked Valerie, "What she would like," she said, "a little book what she can read." Do you know that she can read a book? I am knitting a scarf and do you know that Valerie is doing the same as me? she is doing two plain and two purl, she has not made one mistake yet, she is good! It is not raining now it is fine for a while, we had a little snow storm this morning, it seems to be coming on now. What do you think Mum? I am an angel in a play in school I wonder whether

S xxxxx
you can find me a
pair of wings
a pair of apiloclass
plain, Will do. It is
a cristmas play
about the birth of
Jesus. I am glad
you have hird from
Auntie millie and
that Fransec has
past for scholarship
I was pleased to have
the orange and apple
from Auntie Gladys
and I will write to
her very soon to
thank her. So
Granny likes to
read my letters
I am glad it gives

her a "little" enjoyment, and I am also pleased that she is better now, and give her my love. There is a little thing I want to ask you. Is there a shelter to keep you safe? does Dad have to walk up to the shop. give him my love as well. Well I must say Good-bye and God-Bless

'Mammy Val's Little Book of Allsorts'

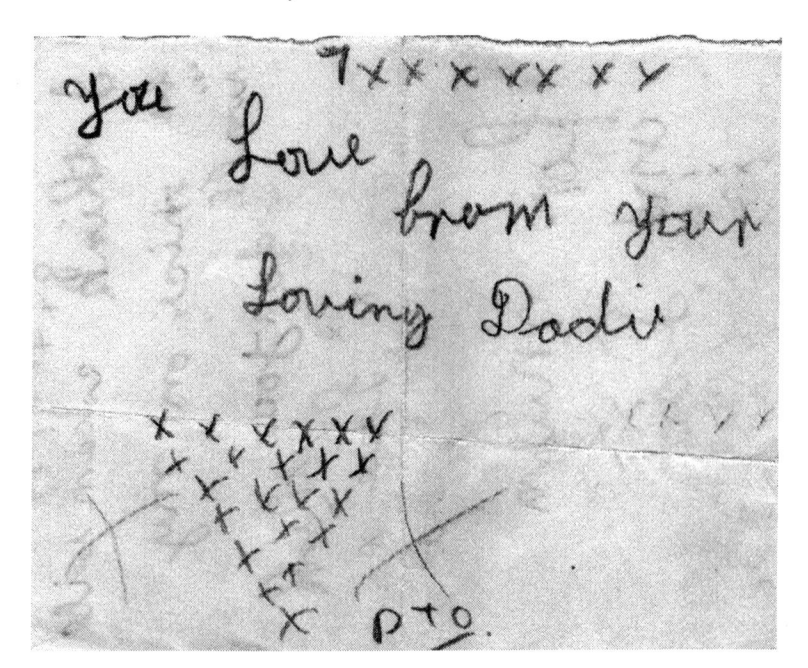

Val Baker Addicott

'Mammy Val's Little Book of Allsorts'

Val Baker Addicott

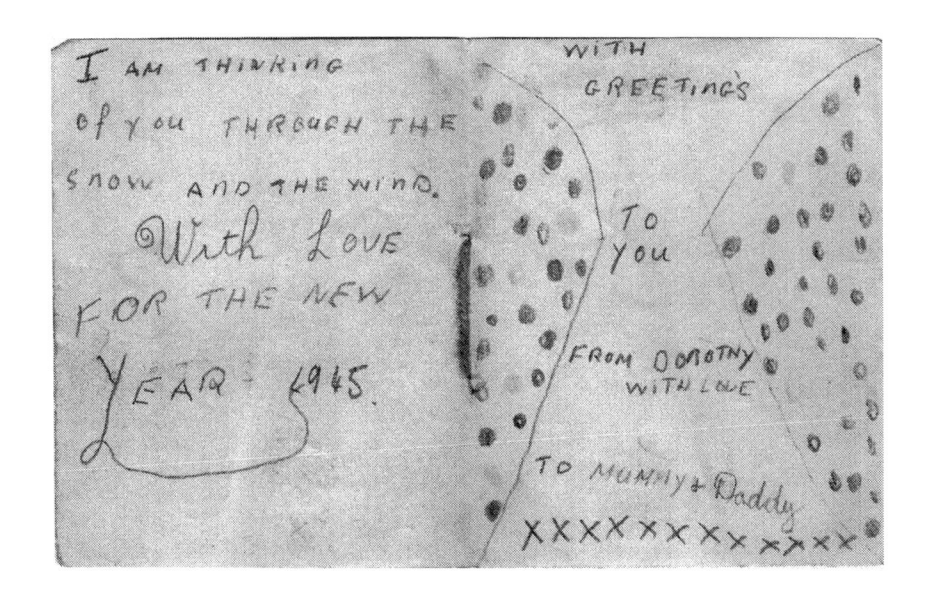

I am thinking of you through the snow and the wind. With Love for the New Year - 1945.

With Greetings to you From Dorothy with love To Mummy + Daddy xxxxxxxxxxxx

'Mammy Val's Little Book of Allsorts'

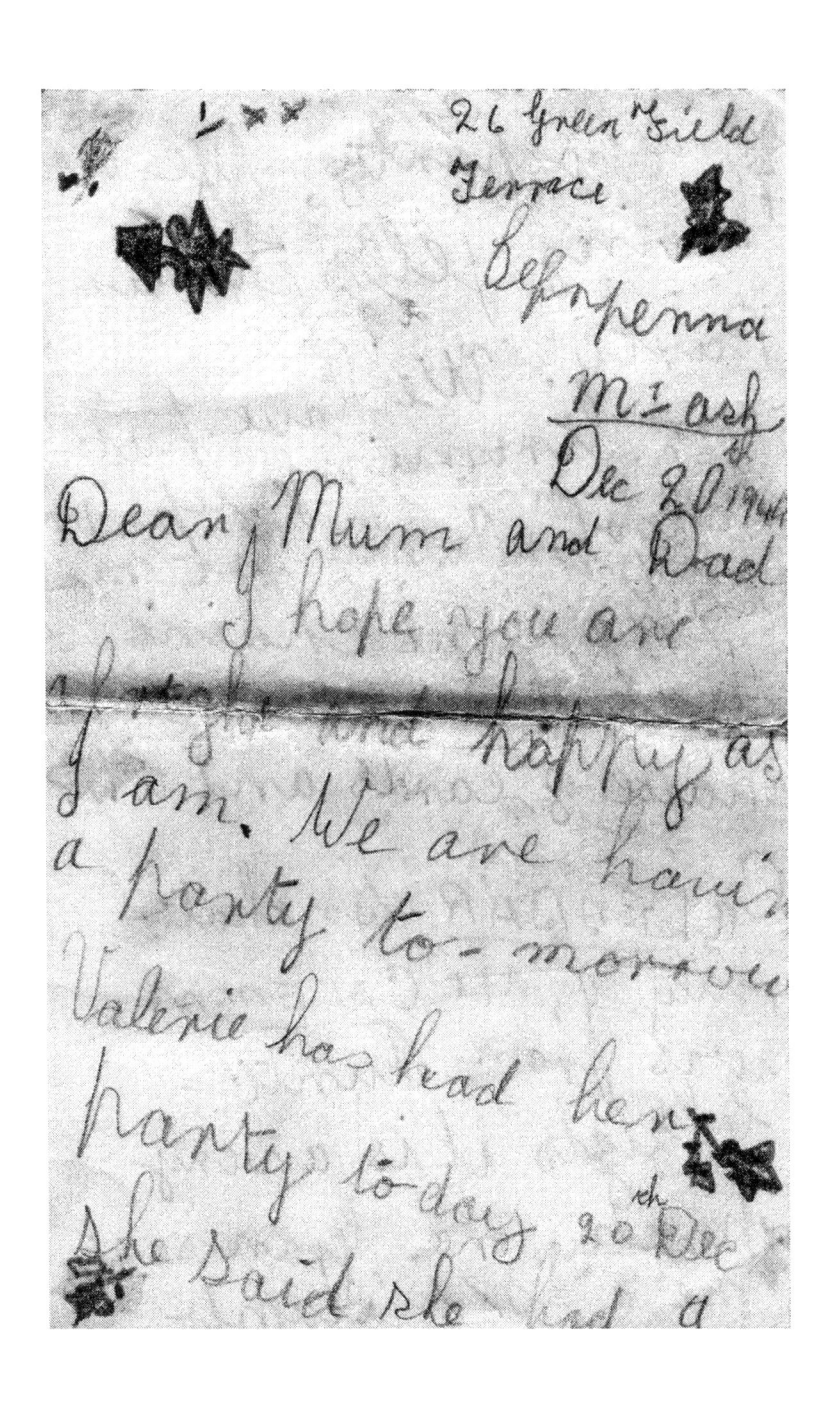

26 Greenfield
Terrace
Cefnpenna
M'ash
Dec 20th 1944

Dear Mum and Dad
I hope you are
alright and happy as
I am. We are having
a party to-morrow
Valerie has had her
party to-day 20th Dec
She said she had a

'Mammy Val's Little Book of Allsorts'

lovely party. We are having jelly for our Party. We have put our triming up in school, Auntie let me take some chains that I made. WE have 8 cards and a CaLENDAR So thats realy 9, the CALENDAR was from Auntie-Glayds it is a very pretty one. Gran sent me a 2/6 stamp that was very Good. of her wasn't. dont tell Grannie I sent her a card. I was very pleased to recieve the lovely card from you and Dad I have got it on the mantle peice and the other with it. I just went down the shop to get oranges and nuts I expect that does make your mouth water does it, they are almon nuts and the Jaffa oranges have

'Mammy Val's Little Book of Allsorts'

You got some you ought too have, Auntie has just given us a roar there Valerie is gone out to crack hers and I am going to crack mine, it was lovely and sweet, I done like to swallow it. I must say good-bye just for now because I have nothing else to say I will wright some more to-morrow about the party when you are going to come, I know you have to do a lot of work, but I would like to see you again. I expect the war will be over in 1946 dont you. Well I must say good-bye and GOD-BLESS YOU.

LOVE FROM YOUR LOVING DAUGHTER
DODIE
OR
DOROTHY
xxxx AND KISSES

21 Greenfield Terr,
Cefnpennar,
Mountain Ash
30ᵀᴴ Dec 1945

Dear Mam & Dad
    I hope you are alright and happy as I am. I wish I could see you again. I hope you recieved my parcel I sent you. I am so sorry I did'nt write before. I had a very happy Cristmas.
    Will you please tell me what time Gran's Bithday I know it is

in Janse but what day do you know. I went to Valerie's nans on Boxing day and had tea there. And Friday we went to the picture to see Make a Wish and B Planes they were both good and lovely I WILL GIVE YOU A LIST OF WHAT I HAD FOR Christ- mas presents some off the Christmas tree & some in my pillow- case. I have just had my tea and we had Blackberry tart and I expect we will soon be having some whimberrie's tarts too. Valerie's Father is comming home Monday, but only for a day. We have still got our trimmings for Mr Barley to see it was lovely when we had the nice fresh holly in the vases we have a lot left but it is a bit shrivveled up I have just finished Auntie Phills hair what I was doing I put it in a sosage roll.

Note: With reference to blackberries and whimberries at Christmas – grandmother bottled them when they were plentiful and always kept some to make tarts at Christmas.

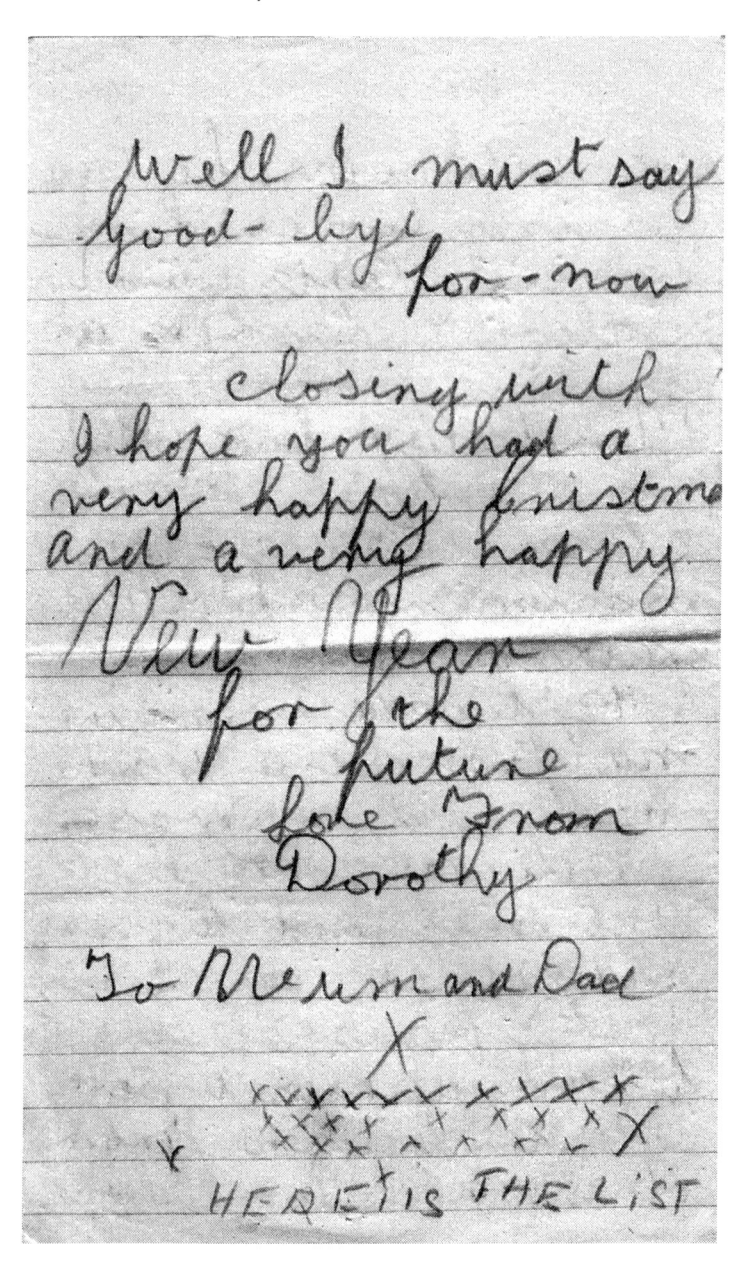

'Mammy Val's Little Book of Allsorts'

Well I must say
good-bye
for-now
closing with
I hope you had a
very happy christmas
and a very happy
New Year
for the
future
love From
Dorothy
To Mum and Dad
X
XXXXXXXXXX
XXXXXXXXXX
HERE IS THE LIST

PS
we had two
cristmas trees
1 big one
~~1 small one~~
1 tiny one

PS
I BROUGHT THE
CRISTMAS TREE
HOME. I SAW SOME
BIG PEICE of FIRE
and I BROUGHT IT HOME
AND AUNTIE PHILL
WAS PLEASED WITH IT
and ALL WAS. SO SHE
TIED THEM ALL together
and MADE A CRISTMAS
TREE THER WERE 4
PEICES. LOVE XXXX

'Mammy Val's Little Book of Allsorts'

Pencil case ⎫ from auntie Glad
Hankie   ⎬
Book   ⎭
Book of Adventure from Aunt Phil
Big book of stories from
          Auntie Phill Auntie
          Gwen Uncle Edwin
A knitting set from Valerie
A pretty needle & thimble case
          from Auntie
                  Phill

Writing book of Christmas tree
pencil of Christmas tree
2 painting books of Christmas tree
1 hanky of Christmas tree
(2) card from Valerie Granny
1/- card of Valerie Auntie Lil
1/- off Mrs Lewis next door
2/6 from Granny
an Orange
an apple
& some nuts.   PTO

PS
we had two
cristmas trees
1 big one
~~1 small one~~
1 tiny one

PS
I BROUGHT THE
CRISTMAS TREE
HOME. I SAW SOME
BIG PEICE OF FIR
and I BROUGHT IT HOME
AND AUNTIE PHILL
WAS PLEASED WITH IT
and ALL WAS. SO SHE
TIED THEM ALL together
and MADE A CRISTMAS
TREE. THER WERE 4
PEICES. LOVE XXXX

26 Grynfield Terr
Cefnpennar
Mountain ash
Jan 6th 1945

Dear Mummy & Daddy
I hope you are very happy as I am. I have just wrote a letter to Auntie Maggie I wrote 1 page and 1 side of another page. We saw a picture lastnight it was called Dr Wosell I enjoyed it very much it took 2 hours it was only 1 picture, still I didnt care because

it was good, Bing Crosby was in the Bing we went to the palace. We are going back to school on Monday because we have had a fortnight's holiday. Valerie is glad it is school on Monday. I am not struck but I don't mind it. Oh! Mum the play went well I didn't have to say anything I only had to sing with Pat Thomas & Maureen O Sullivan We had to sing

Hark The Herald Angels Sing. I have got a card for Grandmama, because I was not sure when her Birthday was I will send it when the 23 comes, she sent me a lovely card for cristmas I supose you saw it. I will be glad of the red candigum and the kanikens there are some holes in them. Well I must close now saying I will be seeing you in the next letter. Well

Good-bye and God-Bless You.
Love From
Doclie

To my Darling Mother + Father
Love & kises

P.S
You couldn't have had a better picture than Dr Wosell.

XXXXXXX
X X X X X X
X X X X X
X X X X
X X X
X
      X

P.S
Dear Mummy,
Hurry up and come hear as I am longing to see you.

Dorothy as a young woman

Val Baker Addicott

D'Alroy Diary

Why Hurry

Life is like a journey: Man, like a train rushing through the night, on lines laid down by circumstance, towards a destination he knows not of:

So why hurry?

At the wish of our parents we arrive at the booking office and we take the ticket that is handed to us:

It seems to be a season ticket for we are always on much the same route.

As we grow older we think that we would like to be different: but how can we?

We are made up of Body, Mind and Spirit – a triad of three moods, a series of compartments; and on we rush.

At times we pick up a new passenger; at times a passenger steps out of our lives;

We are like a train animated by desires, greed, aspirations; even inspirations:

Streaking through the night but why hurry?

The journey has always been just as long and the scheduled running time is still three score years and ten.

Note: Through all the trials and tribulations of her life – 100 years – gran remained loving and kind and I must admit very strong willed but she also had a sentimental streak as it was from her note-book I found these words.

Lately, I appear to have picked-up quite a few passengers and for you all I have compiled this little book. My daughter's young friends are mine and it is a lovely feeling that they all call me 'Mammy Val'.

THE END

Val Baker Addicott

ABOUT THE AUTHORL

I was born in Somerset just before the outbreak of WW2 – when the war escalated my mother and I went to live with my maternal grandmother and her bachelor brother (my Uncle Edwin who replaced my father in my affections and remained there) in the South Wales Valleys. Dorothy had already been evacuated and was living with grandmother. Because of my mother's untimely death and my father's remarriage (never heard again from him after his marriage) I was raised by my grandmother. I married my husband Emlyn Addicott in 1959 and we had two children Phillip and Eryl Lynne (Ella to her friends) My husband's promotion took us to Pembrokeshire in 1971 – grandmother came to and in 1986 reached her 100th birthday.

I had always wanted to write but family ties always kept me busy and it wasn't until after my husband's death in 2007 that I really set-to on my manuscripts to self-publish them all through Create-space a subsidiary of Amazon. If you have enjoyed this 'little' book check out my other books on Amazon – Val Baker Addicott.

Valerie

'Mammy Val's Little Book of Allsorts'

Made in the USA
Charleston, SC
24 September 2014